HAPA TALES
and Other Lies

HAPA TALES
and Other Lies

*A Mixed Race Memoir About
the Hawai'i I Never Knew*

SHARON H. CHANG

RISING SONG PRESS
Seattle

© 2018 by Sharon H. Chang
All rights reserved.

Cover design by Ann Kumasaka

Library of Congress Control Number: 2018953966

ISBN: 978-1-7324847-0-2

Rising Song Press
Seattle, Washington

Printed in the United States of America

This book is especially for Mixed Race people living in liminal state, feeling lonely and landless, yet still asking critical questions about the pursuit of racial justice everywhere. We have a place and purpose in that pursuit too—though it was never destined to be a singularly defined, easily understood, or simple one.

Please keep on. You are brave and needed.

And not alone.

ACKNOWLEDGMENTS

Very first, I must acknowledge that I wrote this book as a non-Indigenous person on Indigenous land. There is a critical Indigenous history of Hawai'i that too often goes unheard. I give deep thanks to the islands and the Native Hawaiian people for the privilege of visiting and have worked throughout this text to weave in the unheard story and pay my respects, knowing that I will always have more work to do in showing up as a true ally to the Sovereignty Movement.

I would like to give immense gratitude to my dear friends the Paks, for inviting me to stay with them on O'ahu and learn more about their family's story as intergenerational Kama'aina artists, activists, and the descendants of Asian plantation workers. Until that point I had only ever experienced Hawai'i as a tourist, which, I now see, had very harmful implications for my understanding, leading me to become way too complicit.

I am so grateful for this book's review panel of three great thinkers whom I also feel honored to call friends. Maile Arvin, brilliant Native Hawaiian professor and inspirational activist. Dawn Rego-Yee, radiant Native Hawaiian and Mixed woman, mother, community advocate, and social worker. And Kenji Kuramitsu, Queer Mixed Yonsei/Gosei writer and change-maker, whose Japanese family goes back five generations in Hawai'i. You gave such invaluable feedback and insight as I was developing this memoir, challenging me to think and go deeper, while also encouraging me when I had self-doubt. This book wouldn't be here today with you.

There are not enough words to express my appreciation for two Seattle women and neighbors who poured their gifts into the production of this beautiful book. Ann Kumasaka, graphic designer and Asian American sister, who generously donated her time and talent to create the gorgeous cover and layout of what you are about to read. Meredith Jacobson, editor extraordinaire, who meticulously and thoughtfully edited this text from start to finish with care, concern, and loving respect. Thank you both for bringing this, my first self-published project, to the professional standard I dreamed of but was told by a male-dominated publishing industry I could never achieve. Linking arms as smart, powerful women—we proved them wrong, didn't we?

As always, dearest thanks to my life partner and confidant, Don Farwell, who continues to let me think out loud and bounce ideas off him, and to always respond with astute questions. As an Asian Mixed man you truly show such profound, interesting, and complicated understandings of the world. I'm grateful every day for your sharp intellect, analysis, and reflections, and that we are spending our lives together.

And finally, as always, thank you to my son, Kazuo Farwell, who is so thoughtful, compassionate, creative, and kind. It's been such a gift watching you grow up with these ideas and to hear your revelations as part of the next youth generation. Frankly, at eight years old, you are already coming up with discerning views I never considered. You open my eyes all the time. I appreciate you letting me share our story with others and can't wait to hear more of your thoughts in the years to come.

CONTENTS

NOTES 2

PREFACE: *Morning* 14

CHAPTER 1: *Lullaby* 20

CHAPTER 2: *Mainland Mixed* 37

ALOHA 47

CHAPTER 3: *Food* 55

CHAPTER 4: *First Gear* 67

HAOLE 81

CHAPTER 5: *Brown* 90

CHAPTER 6: *Roots* 106

HAPA 115

CHAPTER 7: *Paradise* 122

CHAPTER 8: *Blazing* 134

MALIHINI 147

CHAPTER 9: *Waves* 157

CHAPTER 10: *Circle to Center* 174

AFTERWORD: *Home* 189

EPILOGUE 194

SELECTED BIBLIOGRAPHY 196

In our genealogy, Papahānaumoku, "earth mother,"
mated with Wākea, "sky father," from whence came
our islands, or moku. Out of our beloved islands came
the taro, our immediate progenitor, and from the taro,
our chiefs and people … We are stewards of the earth,
our mother, and we offer an ancient, umbilical wisdom
about how to protect and ensure her life … No one
knows how better to care for Hawai'i, our island home,
than those of us who have lived here for thousands
of years.

— HAUNANI-KAY TRASK,
From a Native Daughter:
Colonialism and Sovereignty in Hawai'i

NOTES

For a magnificent two millennia, Hawai'i was inhabited solely by her children, the Kānaka Maoli (true people), and Native Hawaiians created a thriving civilization built upon Indigenous caring for the land. There was no contact with the outside world, no money, and no concept of financial profit during those thousands of years of self-governance. Rather, it was exchange between land-cultivating 'ohana (extended families) that formed the core economy, across a plenitude of island communities with a population numbering almost one million at its peak. Hawai'i was once a cohesive, autonomous and flourishing Indigenous, sovereign nation.

Then the white man arrived. Captain James Cook "discovered" Hawai'i for white people in 1778, and within a century, Kānaka Maoli had been decimated by colonizer-introduced diseases, disenfranchised, and dispossessed, their land taken and tamed, all for the benefit of white supremacy. The Native Hawaiian population was reduced to less than 40,000 by 1890 and their once-thriving civilization was supplanted by a haole (white) planter oligarchy. With the backing of the US military, the last ruling sovereign, Queen Lili'uokalani, was overthrown by haole plantation aristocracy in 1893, and the islands were forcibly annexed into the United States in 1898.

Sugarcane plantations were one of the most lucrative businesses for white colonizers and the primary channel through which Asians would begin to arrive en masse on the islands. The sugar industry was tightly controlled by white missionary families and businessmen, concentrated into a handful of corporations known as the Big Five. White industry in Hawai'i grew just as it did on the continent (on cotton plantations, in building the Transcontinental Railroad, etc.)—on the backs of cheap labor, exploiting increasing numbers of workers with no power and few options. Since the Native population of Hawai'i had been decimated by white-introduced disease, white colonizers looked further afield for labor to exploit.

They found that labor in Asia, which was unstable at the time due to American, European, and Japanese imperialism. White planters enticed vulnerable Asian populations to Hawai'i by offering economic opportunity and a political haven. Once employed, however, Asian immigrant laborers found themselves effectively indentured servants, denied citizenship, suffering under exploitative conditions and horrific anti-Asian racism on the plantations. Whenever the threat loomed of laborers organizing, white planters simply shifted their recruitment efforts, turning first to Chinese, then to Japanese, Korean, and Filipino workforces.

By 1920, whites had lured more than 300,000 Asian laborers to Hawai'i, composing 62 percent of the islands' population. In other words, white people built an Asian-settler majority on Native Hawaiian land. Despite white planters' divisive efforts to maintain an ethnically stratified caste system among this workforce, Asian laborers eventually organized across ethnic lines and merged with ongoing Native Hawaiian resistance to the abusive oligarchy. General strikes, protests, and other acts of civil disobedience persisted, resulting in an eventual overthrow of white minority rule, with the Democratic Party takeover of 1954, and the Big Five losing political and economic control of Hawai'i—a fate that was decisively sealed with statehood in 1959.

But for Kānaka Maoli, statehood would become just the latest villain in a long occupation, further dispossessing them from their ancestral lands, ripping them from the arms of their mother. Statehood meant full induction into US capitalism and profit-driven commercial interest. The Democratic Party failed to resolve Native Hawaiian claims for land and demands for return to self-governance. In the late 1960s, rising investment by multinational corporations instead resulted in the rapid takeover of agricultural areas and eviction of Native Hawaiians from their remaining rural communities. A new tourist economy that pushed urbanization and development, especially of hotels, came to dominate the second half of the twentieth century and has entered the twenty-first with guns blazing. Today, it is foreign investors, big business, and the state of Hawai'i that lure outsiders to the islands with promises of palm trees and a postracial paradise replete with welcoming hula girls in lovely shades of brown to help you forget racism ever existed.

The multibillion-dollar corporate tourist industry, colonizer-run, continues to be backed by the US military, which has occupied Hawai'i since the overthrow of Queen Lili'uokalani, confiscating hundreds of thousands of acres of Native land for military use. Post–World War II, Hawai'i has become a center for American forces in the Pacific and one of the most militarized of the many places US imperialism has colonized across that vast ocean.

Meanwhile, new settlers of color and descendants of Asian plantation workers, particularly of Japanese and Chinese heritage, have been able to ascend in Hawaiʻi by participating in this same colonial system of violence, benefiting from the large-scale disenfranchisement of the lands' Indigenous people, and sometimes even becoming colonial agents themselves. As revolutionary Hawaiian nationalist Haunani-Kay Trask writes in "Settlers of Color and 'Immigrant' Hegemony: 'Locals' in Hawaiʻi":

> For our Native people, Asian success proves to be but the latest elaboration of foreign hegemony. The history of our colonization becomes a twice-told tale, first of discovery and settlement by European and American businessmen and missionaries, then of the plantation Japanese, Chinese, and eventually Filipino rise to dominance in the islands.

Native Hawaiians have always resisted, and continue to resist, their violent occupation. When Queen Liliʻuokalani was forcibly deposed and placed under house arrest, she gave in only under great protest, demanding that the US reinstate her rightful sovereignty. In 1897, more than 21,000 Native Hawaiians—more than half the Hawaiian and part-Hawaiian population—signed the Kūʻē (opposition) Petition against US annexation. And in the last fifty years, Indigenous Hawaiians have been advocating the return of lands and self-government, in what is now known as the Hawaiian Sovereignty Movement.

ABOUT THE LANGUAGE

Hawaiian words are not italicized in this book, because setting words apart in italics is a way of continuing to frame not only the Hawaiian language but also the Native Hawaiian people as "foreign" and "unassimilable" in a place that is rightfully theirs. Alienating language and people in this manner is a longstanding practice of settler colonialism; it's often found in writing out of the West and is a practice that, as the child and daughter-in-law of Asian immigrants as well as a settler of color, I fully reject.

It also needs to be stated unequivocally that the concepts of "local" and "mainland" are fraught with difficulty. In Hawai'i, "local" is an identity used to distinguish between those who reside on the islands (whether Hawaiian, Asian, Mixed, haole, etc.) and those who do not. The idea of a "local nation-state" originally arose in the seventies as resistance to white settler colonialism as well as commercial overdevelopment on the islands. But "local" is also an identity that has been used to obscure the dominant political power of modern resident Asians and haoles—a power that continues to deeply subjugate the Native Hawaiian peoples. As Haunani-Kay Trask points out:

> Today, modern Hawai'i, like its colonial parent the United States, is a settler society. Our Native people and territories have been overrun by non-Natives, including Asians.

> Calling themselves "local," the children of Asian settlers greatly outnumber us. They claim Hawai'i as their own, denying indigenous history, their long collaboration in our continued dispossession, and the benefits therefrom.

Similarly, "mainland" is often used in Hawai'i to refer to the forty-eight adjoining US states on the North American continent (excluding Alaska and Hawai'i). Again, meant to draw bright geographic cultural distinctions by so-called locals, this reference also becomes harmfully anti-Indigenous in that it refers to the contiguous United States as the "main" body rather than centering Hawai'i and its Native peoples. Worse, normalizing the term in dominant use pushes a colonizer mindset upon Native Hawaiians and encourages feelings of inferiority that have been internalized by Kānaka Maoli. In sum, neither "local" nor "mainland" centers Native Hawaiians.

At the same time, "local" and "mainland" are incredibly common reference points in Hawai'i and an inescapable part of everyday rhetoric. The words are so embedded in daily use, in fact, that to throw them away would be to ignore a cornerstone of Hawai'i's current social psyche, albeit a problematic one. So, to indicate the commonality of the concepts yet simultaneously hold them in tension, the two words will always appear in quotation marks or within a quoted reference.

I have also capitalized certain identifying terms, such as Mixed, Brown, Indigenous, Biracial, Queer—some you may not be used to seeing capped. I capitalize these terms, again, to bring forward and center people typically marginalized. Likewise, I do not hyphenate racial identities because the hyphen has been conspicuously applied to some groups (such as "Asian-American" or "mixed-race") in ways that disrupt our wholeness by framing us as disparate pieces linked through punctuation.

And finally, on the appropriation of the Hawaiian word "hapa" by non-Hawaiian Mixed people. I have used "hapa" in the title of this book only so it will appear in reader searches—a necessary evil in the age of technology, information overload, and keyword searchability. This problematic usage in the title is intentional. Within this book, for the reasons described above, when referring to non-Hawaiian people I use the word "hapa" only in quotation marks or in quoted material. As Native Hawaiian scholar Maile Arvin explained to me, hapa was conceived in the Hawaiian language not just to describe Hawaiian Mixed peoples, but to resist and thrive by claiming Hawaiian Mixed children strongly into an ʻohana that had been almost wiped out by settler colonialism. Over time the term has evolved in Hawaiʻi to describe any Mixed person, which is perhaps acceptable when it at least occurs on Native Hawaiian land, in a context where others hopefully have some knowledge of Native Hawaiian people.

Nonetheless, currently many non-Hawaiian Mixed people all over the world, especially those of partial Asian descent, are claiming "hapa" identity ahistorically for themselves in trying to resolve their anxiety about not-belonging where they are. The excuse for their

8

taking is often simply that language travels and evolves. But there are many nuanced problems with this choice and rationale, as Nora Okja Keller aptly expressed in her essay "Circling 'Hapa'":

> Reflexively, almost as soon as I meet someone, I explain: "I am hapa." I say it definitively, "I am hapa," as if that statement, self-explanatory, says it all. But really, it doesn't. It's superficial, an easy way out.

> [I]n Santa Barbara, I met a woman who was half-Latina and half-Japanese. "I am *hap-pa*," she announced, spelling the word for me. When I told her that in Hawai'i, we spell hapa with one "P," she said, "What's Hawai'i got to do with it? Isn't *happa* the Japanese word for half breed?"

Claiming a "hapa" identity without regard or respect for its Native history and without making a commitment to show up in perpetuity for the Hawaiian Sovereignty Movement is, to my mind, still a co-optation that is complicit in settler colonial erasure of Indigenous peoples. There is also a need to speak directly to power and point out that dominant culture *encourages* those of us who are non-Native to become politically apathetic "hapas" precisely because it upholds the white supremacy and settler colonialism built upon the backs of Native Hawaiian suffering. This controversy is something I have discussed at length in essays and in my first book, *Raising Mixed Race: Multiracial Children in a Post-Racial World*, and will continue to discuss here.

As a non-Native Asian Mixed woman who is often falsely assigned Hawaiian identity and seen as acceptably "hapa" when Native Hawaiians themselves are not allowed the same on their own ancestral lands, I feel I have an especial responsibility to call out the colonial systems that keep Indigenous people oppressed. If I remain silent while benefiting from wedge politics and "happy hapa" stereotypes, I am an accomplice.

What follows here, through the lens of my latest visit to Oʻahu and Kauaʻi, is a chapter of my identity story, one that specifically questions a lifetime of formative Hawaiʻi memories funneled to me through pop culture and visits to the islands as a tourist. Certainly, this is part of a larger, necessary story about the loneliness and challenge of self-defining that Mixed Race people generally face in a racist yet monoracially aligned society.

But this is also the story of how, in my personal search for rooted belonging in a multiracial body, I was misled by colonialist narratives my entire life to believe, as an Asian Mixed girl and woman, that I could find that belonging in a settler myth about Hawaiʻi. It is the story of how, in my intense desire to see others like me and belong somewhere, anywhere, I ultimately *allowed* myself to be misled, becoming an abettor to colonialism at the expense of Hawaiʻi and her children, the Kānaka Maoli. And in the end, this is the story of how I have begun a new chapter in which I challenge myself to keep searching for a transformative Mixed-Race identity that is not built upon the oppression of others.

It must be acknowledged that in this storytelling I have advantages, being a light-skinned person of East

Asian and white descent, a Mixed woman who fits a dominant stereotype, born and raised entirely on the continent. I face fewer consequences for speaking and *can* speak because colonizer and settler readers will feel more comfortable with me in this body I inhabit. Throughout this book, I endeavor always to be aware of my privilege where it exists and try not to write in ways that would harm Native Hawaiians. I am not, nor am I attempting to be, an expert on Hawai'i in any way. This text should not be an endpoint for anyone; I encourage you to explore the sources listed in my bibliography at the end of this book. All readers should seek out the works, words, and activism of Native Hawaiians who are doing truly brilliant things in the world.

There were riots in Honolulu last week between sailors on leave and what they described in ill-tempered words as "gooks—that stupid, shoeless, dirty lower strata of Honolulu citizen." The riots, however, marked only a small failure in what is otherwise the world's most successful experiment in mixed breeding, a sociologist's dream of interracial cultures.

— *LIFE* MAGAZINE,
Nov. 26, 1945

Morning

It's dark morning. Early. Clock ticking. Brain whirring. That first cup of coffee tastes so damn good. Second or third cups never taste right. I don't know why. There's not much I like more than early, dark, quiet mornings with my thoughts, my piles of books, my writing.

In a few weeks we're going to Hawai'i, and I'm thinking about my last visit, to Kaua'i, all those years ago. Oh, man. Those were some of the best early dark mornings. Just me and the soon-to-be husband in a little yellow house across the street from a little beach.

He doesn't get up early. He's a night owl. Which works for us. It's just me, and it's good knowing he's sleeping nearby. Then the wet, warm air sitting with me like an old, soft blanket. The sound of the ocean, the rhythm of her movement, an old familiar friend. And the chickens. Which sounds stupid and was, kind of, at first. But quickly, easily, their cluckings and crowings just became part of it all. I don't remember anymore what I thought, read, or wrote, those early mornings in Kaua'i all those years ago. *Did I write?* But I remember the air, the sounds, the ocean, the chickens.

Now it's so many years later. I'm different and the same person. My early dark Seattle morning is fading to light. *Don't leave yet.* Someone's beeping to get into their car, and I already feel exhausted by the city, the people, the day ahead of me. Midday, I'll be speaking with a families-of-color group about antibias early learning and finding the right childcare fit for their infants. Tonight, I'm covering a public forum for Tommy Le, the young Vietnamese American man who was shot and killed by King County police in June. *No parent should have to outlive their child,* I remember they said when my high-school prom date died in a plane crash. What an intense thing, I'm realizing, to go in one day from the hope and excitement of new motherhood to the sudden loss of a son, the squelching of parental hope and promise, by racism and police brutality. It will be heavy, hard.

And all of it brings me back to Hawai'i again—a place forcibly taken by racism, violence, and white supremacy, like so many others—the same supremacy built everywhere upon the backs of Indigenous expropriation and genocide. Hawai'i. A place where Native peoples have been decimated to fractions by whites, but where Asian and Mixed Race people are the modern majority. Hawai'i. A place where it's often assumed I belong because of this Asian Mixed racialized body of mine; where I'm part of the story even when I'm not. Hawai'i. A place that seems doggedly determined to live inside a tailored post-racial island fantasy that, though now perpetrated largely by Asian and Mixed folk, remains entirely white supremacist, anti-Indigenous and anti-Black.

But they tell me I don't know. I'm not "local." I don't understand. I could never understand. And perhaps that's true.

The day is brighter and brighter. The orange light of the rising sun is cutting through the kitchen window, hitting the cabinets in geometry, lines and angles, speckled by the shadows of tree leaves. In the last decennial census, nine million people reported they were Mixed Race. Of those nine million, 92 percent reported they were Biracial and 75.5 percent reported they were "part white," like me. Of those nine million, the largest overall number were in California (where I'm from), and the largest percentage of a state population were in Hawai'i (where I'm about to go). Specifically, Honolulu was the place with the highest proportion of people reporting mixed-white, mixed-Asian, and mixed-Hawaiian/Pacific Islander identities.

So you'll understand when I say that, even though I'm not from the islands and have never lived there, who I am as an Asian Mixed person has still always been filtered through the prism of Hawai'i. Because the place where there are the most people who look like me, in a settler colony where so few look like me, is Hawai'i. Because others connect me to the islands whether I ask them to or not. Because there's a mirage, a story about people who look like me, that comes from this place.

Being Mixed Race in a highly racialized, fissured, and fractured society is often about searching for where we belong. But belonging within division is complicated and painful, and our desperate search for it easily goes astray.

Too often I see people who look like me cling to a complicit identity that is dead asleep, willfully blind, and hurtful to us as well as others. That complicit identity is modeled after a settler trope born in Hawai'i: a model multiracial narrative about Mixed people that furthers the oppression of Native Hawaiian people there and is increasingly used on the "mainland" to further the oppression of Black and Brown people here. It goes like this: *Racism isn't real because Mixed People of Color have succeeded by not rocking the boat. If Black and Brown people would just "behave" like that, things would be good for them too.*

Which means Hawai'i is a particular place where folks like me, whether "local" or "mainland," should be thinking long and hard about our mixedness within the context of settler colonialism, stolen land, Indigenous struggles, anti-Black and -Brown racism.

But I don't know that we do.

So,

I wait to return.

Maybe something?

Maybe nothing.

Maybe everything.

Even then I'll remain a tourist, which means, rightfully so, whatever I experience gives me no authority over the land and its people. At the same time, returning is a critical chance to look back at a lifetime tied to this string—albeit a thin one—that always seems to connect me to this place. I think, as an Asian Mixed woman returning to Hawai'i, this is an opportunity to dig very, very deep into Who I Am and how Who I Am is continually built upon an intricacy of oppressions and privileges.

And from that reflection,

I think I must,

I need

to go even deeper.

In our language, "koa" is not used to describe those who fight in battles because it means "warrior"; it is used to describe those who fight in battles because it means "brave." It means "courageous." It is connected to the mighty koa tree ... To grow through pain, sometimes from being broken, and then to give so generously of yourself, that is bravery and that is courage. That is koa.

— BRYAN KAMAOLI KUWADA,
"We Are Not Warriors. We Are a Grove of Trees" (2015)

There's a sunny little, funny little melody
That was started by a native down in Waikiki
He would gather a crowd down beside the sea
And together they'd play his gay Hawaiian Chant
Soon the other little natives started singin' it
And the hula hula maidens starting swingin' it
Like a tropical storm that's the way it hit
Funny little gay Hawaiian chant.

— "HAWAIIAN WAR CHANT,"
by Johnny Noble and Ralph Freed (1936)

CHAPTER ONE

Lullaby

Seems none of us can help falling in love with the new big-studio musical. It's designed to strum our heartstrings, sweep us away with romantic song. But part of me feels maybe manipulated. So I read the words of a geographer at the National Museum of the American Indian: "Another depiction that is tiresome and cliché is the happy natives with coconuts trope." Oh. "Coconuts as the essential component of Pacific Island culture became a comedy staple on the 1960s television series Gilligan's Island, *if not before." I suddenly recall that I watched* Gilligan's Island *devotedly as a child and loved it like the big-studio musical now. In fact, I still remember the lyrics to the show's theme song. But somehow, I don't remember the coconuts...*

In third grade my Asian Mixed husband was picked to sing "Hawaiian War Chant" in a year-end program for parents at his mostly white elementary school. Every morning throughout the year, third graders at his school would practice singing different songs, many of them from white musicals like *Chitty, Chitty, Bang, Bang*. White teachers would walk the room, lean down and listen, carefully assess, nodding their heads when children sang admirably. They pointedly asked my husband, eight-year-old Asian Mixed boy, to audition for the war chant solo. He won out against a white boy and, in the final program, sang to a primarily white audience accompanied by a white hippy playing conga drums. He still knows the Hawaiian chorus word-for-word to this day:

> Tahuwai la a tahuwai wai la
> Ehu hene la a pili koo lua la
> Pututui lu a ite toe la
> Hanu lipo ita paalai
> Au we ta huala
> Au we ta huala

But those original lyrics by a Kānaka Maoli have nothing to do with war. They were haole-appropriated from a Native Hawaiian love song, "Kāua I Ka Huahua'i," written by Prince Leleiohoku in 1860. The love song became the misleadingly named hit "Hawaiian War Chant" in 1936 when Johnny Noble, a white bandleader at the Moana Hotel on Waikīkī Beach, decided to create a jazzed-up adaptation for entertainment. Noble's interpretation was popularized even further through versions recorded on the continent by artists like Tommy Dorsey, Spike Jones, and even Ella Fitzgerald. "Hawaiian War Chant" features prominently in Disney's Enchanted Tiki Room and was even sampled by virtual band Gorillaz on their album *The Fall*.

My husband and I, as adults, have laughed painfully about this story more than once. In hindsight, it does seem implausibly funny. Anyway, what else is there to do at this point? It happened. Laugh or cry, I guess. When it comes to our son, who is at the moment also eight years old, however, the laughing instantly disappears. *Whoosh.* Vacuum-sealed, banished from our minds. The recollection doesn't seem even slightly funny anymore. Our faces settle sternly, seriously, ferociously when we imagine what we would do if our boy found himself in the same situation. We both agree, there is no fucking way *we* would ever allow our son to be tokenized like that. Ever.

Local. Tourist. "Hapa." Haole.

Imposter.

Belonging has always seemed so elusive to me in this place called America.

Asian.

Biracial.

Mixed.

Woman.

Mother.

Partner.

Writer.

Activist.

Artist.

Am I American? I'm American, my official documents declare. But this place where I was born, this stolen landscape, even as it's overwritten again and again, was still never written with someone like me in mind. Bodies like mine live in liminal state, landless, adrift. Bodies like mine are affixed, fashioned to the prow of their ships, the ones that never seem to stop sailing, ailing the back of the sea as they force her to carry their vessels to distressed shores. And as they keep breaking and taking the land, it suits to appropriate a face like mine as their sickly-sweet figurehead: part somewhere-that's-not-here, part nowhere, part "them."

———◆———

I go to the public pool once a week, usually on Friday, when my son is in school. It's a time when some serious swimmers work out, like me, but mostly diverse elders from Seattle's south-end community show up to rehabilitate or exercise in the ways they can. In this weekday, midday context, the spa becomes a revealing social microcosm. As we swimmers sit in the hot tub, trying to relax, we are involuntarily positioned face-to-face. And in such close quarters, elders strike up conversations—about their lives, memories, politics, the city, current events—simply because it's awkward to be in silence.

On the one hand, the conversations that unfold among this racially diverse group of elders—who hold the stories of our past and the keys to remembering it—are a fascinating lesson in sociopolitical history. On the other hand, it's in this place that I become again what I haven't been since I was a younger woman: a magnet for white men with Asian fetishes. But now they're older men. It's gross. Especially as we're all in our bathing suits, in a hot tub, and they have decades on me. But gendered Asian fetishes have always been gross. So, nothing new.

It typically begins with the men palpably staring, at which point it's clear they're about to zero in. A conversation with me is subsequently started, and sooner or later some racialized gender sewage bubbles to the surface. Usually sooner. Like the time an old white man rudely interrupted my conversation with another person to insert, "So, Sharon, what do you do? Are you a flight attendant?"

There was also the old white man who insisted on asking me questions about myself, and when I gave only guarded answers, he did instead what he'd likely intended to do all along: he launched into a narcissistic diatribe about his just-right-of-left politics, his easy military career (since he was a West Point graduate, he rose the ranks quickly), his current contract with the government manufacturing custom guns, and his Asian wife, whom he described as a "professional nanny."

Then there was the old white guy who just had to tell me about his hot music-industry career back in the day, and how, as an A&R rep, he'd spent a lot of time living out his island fantasies in Hawai'i. By his description, Hawai'i "back then" had been something of a tropical Burning Man, blissfully breezy, easy, and bohemian. He boasted about the parties he went to, the good times he'd had, about hanging out with legends like Jimi Hendrix (and how he knew things about Hendrix that others never knew).

"Though the islands aren't what they were," he reminisced, stars in his eyes, looking over at me for affirmation. He didn't mean what the 'āina (land) was pre-overthrow, when it was stewarded by its Kānaka children for almost two millennia. He just meant what it was for him, in his younger haole heyday. And I know he just had to tell *me* because of my Asian Mixed woman's body, the "right" kind of body, light-skinned part-white, long wet brown hair—the kind of body that has been used to justify white men's control over the islands through sexual fantasy. I hate that my body represents that to him. That I don't matter because his fantasies matter more. But there's nothing I can do other than excuse myself. *I've got to go pick up my son*, is always my excuse. *Have a good one.*

Orchestral music swells as two swimmers, a young white man and an Asian Mixed woman, make their way underwater beneath a coral reef into a sequestered ocean pool where the woman's Asian mother awaits, grinning, upon a rock. The young couple settle in beside her. They sit facing one another, surrounded by tropical flora and mist (or is it steam?). The setting is heated, romantic, and idyllic.

"*Happy, Lieutenant?*" *asks the pleased mother, laughing joyously as she strokes the wet hair of her exquisite but wordless progeny. The daughter doesn't speak English, so the mother speaks for her. Face falling, she tells the lieutenant that a wealthy French planter—whom the mother dislikes—has been asking repeatedly to marry her daughter.*

"*You can't let her marry a man like that!*" *protests the Lieutenant.*

"*He's a white man too,*" *points out the mother, "and very rich.*"

"*I don't care!*" *the Lieutenant protests in a fit of passion. "You can't let her marry him!*"

"*Okay,*" *says the mother slowly, leaning in. "Then you marry her.*"

The daughter, lei draped around her neck, wet dress clinging to her skin, listens but simply blinks, uncomprehending, as the two discuss her fate.

"*Lieutenant,*" *cajoles the mother sweetly. "You have good life here. Since war I make two thousand dollar! War go on, I make maybe more. Give all the money to you and Liat. You no have to work. I work for you. All day long you and Liat play together. Make love. Talk happy. No think about*

Phil-a-delia. It's no good!"

The lieutenant is staring intensely and rather helplessly at the daughter. It is the perfect moment. The mother bursts into song, orchestra swelling again, as her daughter, framed by long, wet brown hair, begins to dance with her hands and arms. Perhaps it is hula, except something doesn't seem quite right. The daughter remains mute but smiles prettily, hopefully, as she sweeps up the heart of a hopelessly enchanted lieutenant. He is smitten. She never utters a word. They kiss passionately.

And in the end, he never will marry her.

As I'm writing this manuscript, Mixed mama of a Mixed boy in 2017, everyone's all about the new animated Disney musical *Moana*. The movie centers Pacific Islander characters (voiced by a color-conscious cast) and the Pacific Islands for the first time. It's shiny and dazzling, a ginormous hit, though I have no idea if it genuinely honors the truths of Pacific Island peoples. It is a Disney movie, after all, which was still helmed by white people. Which, anyway, is kind of a thing in movie musicals.

I know.

When I was a child, I loved watching musicals too. But I watched the early ones, the genre-makers, the classics, which had been a pop-culture staple of my white grandparents' youth. In photos taken during their heyday, 1940s and 1950s actresses like Shirley Jones and Debbie Reynolds remind me so much of my beloved Grammy: cute and snazzy, dressed to the nines, hair coiffed in ever-perfect waves, as middle-class white women were expected to appear in those times.

I remember sitting at night on my grandparents' bed with my sister, in our nightgowns, watching Grammy painstakingly roll and pin the curlers under her hair; she would sleep in them all night to produce faultless curls next morning. She wore curls to her very last day, even when she needed wigs because she got too sick.

My slippery Asian Mixed hair, on the other hand, never did hold curls very well. Except for that one time my mom had it permed like Annie into a giant pompom exploding with spirals when I was maybe seven years old. When I look back at pictures of that perm, puffy and pillowing around my grinning little Asian Mixed face, I am totally mystified. I have no idea what my mother was thinking. I looked so ridiculous and strange.

Likely I don't need to tell you that movie musicals of the Golden Age were very, very white. As the Mixed Race child of a white mother, I was proffered the stuff uncritically and internalized its white-norming without question. It wasn't until only recently, as an almost-middle-aged adult, that I finally recognized this white-dominant messaging and began to unpack it. And as I have done so, I'm also consciously recognizing for the first time that Mixed people like me did appear in some of these white movies: Yul Brynner in *The King and I*, Nancy Kwan in *Flower Drum Song*, and, notably, France Nuyen in *South Pacific*. They were there. They appeared. But only in troubled ways that I now see had inescapable implications for me, the Mixed girl watching.

Filmed on location in Kaua'i and Ibiza with aerial views of Fiji and possibly Malaysia, *South Pacific* was a 1958 romantic island drama based on the Rodgers and Hammerstein musical of the same name, in turn based on James Michener's short-story collection *Tales of the South Pacific*, chronicling his perspective as a white naval officer in World War II. The movie blatantly shows how Asian Mixed women and girls like me are seen as connected to Hawai'i in white peoples' eyes, even when we grow up and live far away from it. As a child, I didn't consciously process these gendered and racialized messages. They were received, filed, and archived, and they became embedded in my sense of self.

Set in the South Pacific during World War II, the movie follows white characters as they discover and supposedly unpack their racism through interracial love against, ironically, the backdrop of US imperialism. White WAVE officer Nellie (Mitzi Gaynor) falls in love with wealthy French planter Emile (Rossano Brazzi) but is unsure if she can marry him because then she would have to stepmother his two Mixed Race children by a deceased islander wife. And white Lieutenant Cable (John Kerr) has a white girlfriend back home but is riddled by guilt and doubt when he suddenly finds himself falling in love with Liat (France Nuyen), the Brown daughter of a local Tonkinese trader.

I always felt perplexed by *South Pacific* as a kid. It was supposed to be one of the first movies to talk about racism in honest and important ways. But as a Mixed child seeing people who looked like me act as mirrors for white peoples' revelations, I didn't find the film revelatory at all. I watched it and avoided it at the same time. I wanted to like it but didn't really. I had no idea actress France Nuyen was a Mixed Woman with an Asian father and white mother, like me, until just recently. When I was a kid, because the movie wanted it this way, I saw Liat as the familiar trope: a radiant, foreign Asian lady who can't speak English and is therefore at the mercy of white men around her.

The hard truth is, France Nuyen could not be allowed to play a Mixed woman onscreen. She needed to unquestionably appear the Brown love interest of a confused white man so the movie could congratulate itself for having white characters ask important questions about their racism. If Nuyen had played her real-life self, a Vietnamese French woman who would go on to earn a Master's degree in clinical psychology, starting a second career as a counselor for abused women and children and women in prison—that would never have worked. For the movie's white gears to grind, Nuyen needed to sit silently in a tide pool, stunning and exotic, doing hula hands to the racist song "Happy Talk," so Lieutenant Cable could navigate toward personal epiphany via enraptured love.

There is no liberation for Liat, as Cable subsequently dies, leaving her to marry another white man whom she doesn't love.

By telling contrast, the children of white planter Emile do appear as Mixed Race onscreen, expressly to allow a white woman success in *her* marriage. The children function as the youthful Mixed bodies Nellie doesn't know if she can love because of their dead Brown mother. A mountain to summit, the children provide the perfect multiracial plot device for Nellie's character development, showing how she ultimately overcomes her prejudice to attain what Liat could not: engagement to a white man and happily-ever-after. It didn't fully register, in my childhood, that bodies like mine were stepping stones for this film and that Nellie didn't want to love Emile specifically because of her racism toward his children, who were like me.

That registers now. Sometimes I'm surprised that no one ever had a frank conversation with me about this movie. Sometimes I puzzle why my white mother would let me consume its racist self-hating shit? But really, I also now know the painful answer to that question: that, in her willfully ignorant parenting, my white mother showed me how she too was unconsciously harboring implicit bias like Nellie's, but perhaps against her own family and birth daughter, me.

A 1960 red MGB crests the hill and drives across the grass, parking a short way in. Elvis and his Hawaiian girlfriend unload the car, wrap their arms around each other, and walk to a ridge that looks out upon a breathtaking view of Honolulu. The lovers settle in for lunch.

"Your grandmother packs a pretty picnic," Elvis observes, peering into the basket his girlfriend is unpacking. Then, marveling, "Boy, the difference between your family and mine!"

"We're not our families," the Hawaiian girlfriend advises sagely. "We're what we make of ourselves."

"You know, you're right," Elvis returns seriously. "If I'm going to make anything of myself, it's about time to get started and take hold of things … I've got to get a job."

"And I gather not in your father's pineapple plant?" prompts the Hawaiian girlfriend.

"No, ma'am," scoffs Elvis. "No red carpet where everyone knows who I am … Hawai'i has a big future. I want to become a part of it. I'm young and healthy, I'm not too stupid."

The Hawaiian girlfriend lays her hand reassuringly on his arm. "You're wonderful."

Elvis becomes impassioned. "This place is growing by leaps and bounds. There are more tourists coming here than any other state in the union." He suddenly lights up. "Hey, that's it!" Motioning at his Hawaiian girlfriend, he says, "I'm glad you thought of it."

The Hawaiian girlfriend is bewildered. "What'd I think of?"

"Tourist business!" exclaims Elvis. "Your business! It's booming, isn't it?"

"It's getting bigger all the time," the Hawaiian girlfriend confirms.

"Well, I know every inch of these islands, I'd make a good tourist guide," Elvis enthuses.

"You'd make a great tourist guide!" the Hawaiian girlfriend cheerfully agrees. She reaches out to sweetly, lovingly touch Elvis again.

But Elvis doesn't have time now. On fire with new ambition, he abruptly pops up and starts running across the grass back to the car, beautiful view and beautiful Hawaiian girlfriend completely forgotten. "I've got to get going!" he declares. "I gotta see your boss, I'm wasting too much time already!"

About to drive off alone, Elvis requires two reminders and two attempts before he finally gets everything packed back in the classy roadster. It's supposed to be funny. His Hawaiian girlfriend is the last thing he remembers.

My sister's favorite musical was *Blue Hawaii*. She was a huge Elvis fan and watched his musicals repeatedly. There were so many. I watched with her, often begrudging, sometimes with interest, and sometimes, yes, even enjoying it.

Elvis Presley made over thirty films throughout his career. *Blue Hawaii* (1961) was the first of three Elvis films shot in Hawai'i, followed by *Girls! Girls! Girls!* (1962) and *Paradise, Hawaiian Style* (1966). Much of *Blue Hawaii* was shot on location at the later-abandoned Coco Palms Resort on Kaua'i, but the film also includes scenes from Waikīkī Beach, Diamond Head, Mount Tantalus, and Hanauma Bay on O'ahu.

Elvis plays Chad Gates, white scion to a Hawai'i pineapple fortune, whose parents expect him to take over the management of the family business, the Great Southern Hawaiian Fruit Company, after returning from military service. But Chad wants to make his own way in the world and instead goes to work as a tour guide at the agency where his girlfriend, Maile Duval, is employed.

My most prominent memories of watching this musical as a young Mixed girl are: a) sensing uncomfortably that I was like the character of Maile in some way I didn't understand or like, and b) thinking that Chad and Maile looked really fake brown. As it turns out, I was right on all counts. In the movie, Maile Duval is supposed to be a Hawaiian French woman, but she was played by white actress Joan Blackman so as not to offend Elvis's white fan base, especially during those pesky interracial kissing scenes. And yes, Presley was apparently so pale before shooting that a producer personally recommended a brand of tanning lamp to darken his skin.

The movie is completely racist, sexist, and anti-Indigenous, riddled with all kinds of appropriative and offensive numbers like "Ku-U-I-Po" and "Ito Eats." In "Rock-a-Hula Baby," backed by an overly enthusiastic band of Brown islander musicians, Elvis sings and gyrates, as was his way, to an audience of primarily rich white folk on his character's estate. At one point in the number, his character, Chad, tosses an ipu to Maile so she'll join in on the gourd drum. As Maile starts to dance too, Chad's snooty white southerner mother (played by Angela Lansbury) clutches her head in horror and proclaims loudly, "I'm going to have a headache—a dreadful headache."

Hawai'i, Hawai'i. Always there somehow. Always a thread, a connection. I'm sorting through my memories as a "mainland" Mixed girl who grew up in so many white places on the continent and lives in one still, and I see Hawai'i always: woven through my field of vision, appearing regularly, sometimes in, sometimes out of reach. I don't belong to the islands and I never will. Yet others see me as belonging to this place more than anywhere else.

The film keeps running, the story keeps telling, the music keeps playing, and it seems I can't be extricated.

And so I can't help but ask what it all means in this Asian Mixed racialized body, as a social-justice writer and activist, in this raced and racist time and place.

In this life, in my work, what is Hawai'i?

Recently I met a new neighbor, a white Jewish woman. She's pretty cool. Funny. Candid. Strong voice. Biting sense of humor and a no-bullshit attitude that feels super East Coast to me. Though I don't know if she's from the East Coast, so I don't say anything about that. But, it will quickly turn out, the same rules of respect and privacy won't apply to her assumptions about me.

We're talking and relating, and I'm thinking, *Damn, I kind of like this woman. Maybe we can be friends.* Then, the million-dollar question: *Can she tell I'm Mixed? I don't think so. Maybe I'm passing.* Because it's complicated and that will matter if we become friends.

I've just decided I am passing for white with this interesting white-lady neighbor, and considering how I feel about that, when she tilts her head suddenly to ask, "Are you from Hawai'i?"

I almost burst out laughing but instead reply with a wry smile, "No. Why do you ask?"

She's getting a little uncomfortable. "Oh, I don't know, just something about the way you talk reminds me of people from Hawai'i." *Uh huh, yeah, right.*

I ask about this authority she has to identify the origins of my speaking cadence: "Are *you* from Hawai'i?"

She's even more uncomfortable. "No, no. I just have a friend from Hawai'i."

This white woman assuming I'm from Hawai'i when I'm not feels othering. Pushing me to identify with a place where Asians, Mixed people, and Pacific Islanders live, rather than the place where I live, has immediately marked my body as racially different and nonwhite. Not unlike how whites assume Asian Americans are foreigners from Asia and can't speak English. It's a reminder. The reminders always come.

I don't know if we'll ever be friends.

Say the word "hula" and images of lithe, brown-skinned maidens, swaying, supple hips, and large, inviting eyes beckon one to a romantic sexual liaison sure to bring erotic delight. These images promote tourism and fill the commercial coffers of multi-national corporations. But for those of us who are practitioners steeped in the ancient form of this Native dance, saying the word "hula" brings forth an enormous cultural matrix from which this sacred dance emerged, connecting us back to our ancestors.

— MOMIALA KAMAHELE,
"*Īlioʻulaokalani: Defending Native Hawaiian Culture,*"
in Asian Settler Colonialism: From Local Governance to
the Habits of Everyday Life in Hawaiʻi, *Candace Fujikane
and Jonathan Y. Okamura, eds. (2008)*

The way she moves her hips
Up to her fingertips
I feel I'm heaven bound
And when she starts to sway,
I've gotta say,
She really moves the grass around.

Although I love to kiss
My little hula miss
I never get the chance
I want to hold her tight
All through the night
But all she wants to do is dance.

CHAPTER TWO

Mainland Mixed

I remember the Brown man, a generation ago, sitting by the side of the road. He was selling coconuts you could drink from with a straw. My parents bought me one and, sipping happily, I felt that coconut was one of the most transcendent food experiences I'd ever had. The thought has never left me. And so I tell my son this story now and I can't help it, I sing a sweet island lullaby. His eyes grow large with awe. He wants a coconut in Hawai'i too. Okay, we'll definitely try, I assure him, smiling as I watch his excitement grow...

It's 2016 and I've just published my debut book about Mixed Race children. Built upon extensive research and interviews with sixty-eight parents, it is the first book to look at the complex task of raising young, multiracial children during a time when post-racial myths about Mixed people abound.

At my Portland book talk there's a small but lovely crowd. We meet at Kinokuniya bookstore in the back of Uwajimaya, an Asian grocery-store chain in the Pacific Northwest. The gracious biracial Asian man who has arranged my book talk is attentive, organized, on point. He loved the book. He lived on the islands, he tells me, and encourages me to make a book-tour stop there. "You should go to Hawai'i."

"Oh, I don't know," I resist uncomfortably. "I get the impression that my book might not have anything to offer to Hawai'i folks." I'm thinking about not-be-longing, not-knowing, but also all the times I've been schooled by Asian Americans who've lived in Hawai'i that things are simply different there from on the conti-nent. My analysis just wouldn't work there, they tell me, because of an Asian-majority population. No compar-ison. Apples and oranges.

I've always taken their word for it.

"No," he repeats earnestly. "You should go. You have a different take on things and could add a lot to the conversation."

I nod and consider, kind of, but really at that point I'm not seriously going to go anywhere.

How much later—a year?—I'm tired, maybe more than a little jaded after receiving a second discour-aging royalty check and realizing my book didn't have the impact I'd hoped it would. I naively believed people would want to uncover the white supremacy and anti-Blackness that can become embedded in Mixed Race identities. Some do. But more do not. Many turn away, wanting instead to hold "multicultural days" so that they can socialize, celebrate, and wear "Happy Hapa" T-shirts they designed themselves.

I'm invited to Skype with a liberal-arts-college class in Olympia that read my book. The instructor appears South Asian. Another gracious, invested, and enthusi-astic reader. I speak to her class through the computer screen.

One student, a young Asian Mixed woman, is from the islands. The book was interesting to her, she concedes, but she fundamentally didn't relate: "I grew up in Hawai'i and it wasn't like this." I assume she's referring to being in the majority, as I've been told before. I get ready to move on.

Then, in almost the same breath, this student suddenly appears to do a 180. She pauses. Out loud she is now acknowledging a kernel of truth in my book and thinking about what it meant, when she was growing up, to "literally live inside a post-racial fantasy" on the islands.

I perk up. Listen. This is different and brave. Seems like I'm about to hear something new. I'm encouraged. *Yes. Let's talk about that post-racial thing. Please, I'd really like to hear you speak on it through the lens of Hawai'i. It's so important.*

But the moment is as fleeting as swallows in a Northwest spring, sweeping low and fast, flashing past—magical and exciting but gone before any real glimpse.

She starts to backpedal, talking again about the "mainland," particularly the Northwest, versus the islands. Inserting that literal and figurative distance between her and here. "I guess," she concludes after a pause, "I can see how it would be hard to be Mixed Race growing up in a place like this, surrounded by whiteness." The loop is closed. I feel disappointed.

Certainly it's hard to know what's happening in this person's mind, and I don't know her life. It's worth considering how rampant the cultural and gendered shaming are when Women of Color speak their minds, particularly when they're revealing family truths. Perhaps there is only so much this student feels she can say in this moment, only so far she feels she can rock the boat, in caring for the good of the whole while so far from home. There is, too, the perception of Hawai'i her mostly white classmates will then take away with them. A lot rides on her representation. That's a heavy load to bear.

The student talks about my book on raising Mixed Race children like it's not her experience at all, like she's a visitor looking in, a tourist viewing from a distance. I can't shake the feeling that she's also distancing herself in doing so. Because at the end of the day she's here too, on the "mainland," a college student in a city that's 83.7 percent white. She chose to be here, in the same place I am, in her Mixed racialized body. I know something about that. I can imagine what her experience has been like so far, and what's to come.

Sure enough, it's not long before rising racial tensions at this same campus make national headlines. A group of students protesting racism at the college are met with accusations of "reverse racism" by a white professor. The conflict escalates and becomes a national debate, culminating in a shooting threat at the college, a multiple-day evacuation, and graduation being moved to an off-campus venue. In an 83.7 percent white city, post–45 election, I'm not surprised. I think about that sister on campus. I think about how she told me she didn't feel impacted by Mixed Race issues and didn't relate to my book because she's from the islands. If we sat down to coffee, talked again now in the privacy of a one-on-one, would she still say the same things to me? Would she still feel distant from it all?

I've finally decided to give it a shot: I'm trying to figure out how to bring my book to Hawai'i. "I believe your book would be a great addition to our festival, which takes place in the first week of May," writes back a well-known Hawai'i woman. I like this woman. She's Mixed too. She's kind, compassionate, understanding, and nice. She's interested. She loops in the festival's director.

But from the start he's unconvinced.

"Is this a big issue in Hawai'i?" he pushes back. "Probably more than half of my acquaintances here are hapa, and this does not seem to be a regular topic of their conversation, at least not in the case of Asians and Hawaiians." Then he admits, "But one can be willfully blind—I worked for many years near Times Square in New York City, and never once noticed a drug deal! Aloha."

What the fuck.

I am instantly wary of this person. Why is he drawing comparisons between Mixed Race issues in Hawai'i and drug deals in New York City? Seems off. I don't think I like him, despite our only communication being by email. But he's a key player, a gatekeeper. My book can't visit without his green light.

She's Mixed, has Mixed children. She's from, and still lives in, Hawai'i. He lives on the islands too. But he's not from there and he's not Mixed, Asian, or Pacific Islander. He's a white man who was educated in England, served in the Royal Marines and Intelligence Corps, and spent the first decade of his editorial career working at prestigious literary companies in New York City.

Thank you, everyone. I think I should clarify some things about my book. First, it's not a parenting book. Though it certainly can be (and has been) read by parents to great benefit. It's actually a sociological study for which I interviewed sixty-eight parents of young multiracial Asian children and discovered that adults tend to be very underinformed and believe vastly disturbing things about race, mixed race, themselves, and their children.

Second, then, it's a book about racism. Not about multiculturalism or ethnicity. That is, it's a look at how mixed race is part of settler colonialism, white supremacy, anti-Indigeneity, anti-Black and -Brown racism, xenophobia, Islamophobia, etc. All of these things I believe have formed, informed, and continue to touch Hawai'i today, yes? For example, the experience of being light-skinned Asian/white would not at all be the same as being brown-skinned Black/Asian. In another example, I critique the use of hapa (indeed I don't use it in the book), which has been very hard for some folks.

And finally, the book problematizes the idea of mixed people as "post-racial" or the end of race. Why? Because it distracts from the reality that we are actually nowhere near solving racism. Think post 9-11 Islamophobia, Black Lives Matter, Flint, Michigan, the upcoming election. The US has always been a very racist nation. I think this would be an interesting conversation to have in Hawai'i, which is often thought of as a post-racial paradise. Is that true? Is there no white supremacy, anti-Indigeneity,

*anti–Black and -Brown racism in Hawaiʻi? And
what is Hawaiʻi's particular relationship to mainland
narratives about postraciality? I hope that helps with
imagining where this book might enter into fascinating dialogue with your communities.*

"Thanks Sharon," she replies attentively. "You're right that your book is different from what I thought based on my initial cursory glances. I think we in Hawaii could definitely challenge perceptions of post-racial utopia."

I like her even more. She knows.

But he's still pushing, pushing, pushing. "Stereotypes via ethnic humor are surely a form of racism, and that can certainly be usefully addressed at the festival (and has been)," he reflects. He's flexing his intellectual and "local" authority. "Current Hawaii fiction by younger writers often address class, ethnic and race issues. But I don't think the mixed race, hapa, phenomenon would have much traction today?"

I perceive what's coming next. Erasure. That every-body's-mixed-so-nobody's-mixed line people love to toe, in gnarled and different ways, when they find the subject of Mixed Race unimportant, superfluous, or threatening.

"Probably 75 percent of our attendees are mixed race, and it's common for people here to boast of the extraor-dinary mixture of their background."

Extraordinary.

Mixture.

"If the issue was focused on mixed-race children, we'd probably have a lot of pointless self-congratulatory rhetoric."

Pointless.

Rhetoric.

"But racism as such is certainly an issue in Hawaii, and very much worth discussing … how it affects who gets to do what—that's worthwhile. Racism as a source of class attitudes and social hostility is … very real here, and not much discussed. Start with the adjectives 'local,' 'haole,' etc."

Local.

Haole.

I don't know what to say anymore to this white man who acknowledges racism yet sees Mixed Race as entirely separate and doubts my ability to contribute anything to a conversation about multiraciality in Hawai'i. I'm starting to get tired. Nevertheless. A response is needed. I sit on it, and my irritation, for some time. I'm frustrated but not ready to entirely give up. Finally, "Yes," I write with restraint. "I can see you still hold a great deal of reservation about my book, work, and its interest/relevance for a Hawai'i readership." I offer to send him the book so he can read it himself.

I send it.

"Mahalo!"

If he just reads it, he'll understand. He'll see.

But he doesn't.

After about a month, another email.

"I did receive your book, thank you," he writes honestly. My heart lifts, rises above ground, ever so slightly. Hope? Understanding? Home? Or, at least, solidarity? No. He's still pushing. No, now he's shoving. "Having read it I can see the problem for multiracial children on the Mainland US, but my view of the issue for Hawai'i hasn't really changed." Oh.

Multiracial.

Mainland.

The email is his longest yet. And he's schooling me, telling me how it is, talking down, taking me down a few notches. "What may be more relevant here in Hawai'i," he instructs, "is how and why multiracial children choose to identify with a particular racial or cultural identity."

Yes, I know. Remember, I'm Mixed and wrote a book about it. My blood starts to boil. I do not take kindly to being instructed on mixedness by a non-Mixed white man, no matter where he resides.

For instance, he continues, "there are many haole (whites) who are part-Hawaiian though you would never know it from looking at them." We call that white-passing, you fool. "Very often they are proud of the fact, and ... proudly invest in knowledge of their Hawaiian ancestry even as they proceed basically as haoles," he tells me. He makes what he apparently considers an apt analogy. "Similarly East Coast people with Indian blood tend to be proud of the fact, while they might conceal that fact if they live in Oklahoma."

I'm stunned—disbelieving and disheartened and angry all at once at this Hawai'i person who tells me my book is too "mainland" yet in the same breath feels his best way to describe a Native Hawaiian Mixed experience (as a non-Native person himself) is by referencing "mainland" Indigenous peoples whom he likely knows very little about.

He goes on.

One particularly interesting example, he expounds, is a current prominent Black Hawaiian actor. *What.*

My spirit, which was steadfastly sinking, becomes completely crushed. *Here we go.* Not only is he dragging Native Americans into this twisted island diatribe, he is also about to add his non-Black view of Blackness. I know exactly where this is going, and it's not going to go well.

"Physically," he observes, this Black Hawaiian actor "reads as Black, powerful voice, with the tall, imposing physique of a professional Black basketball player." *Basketball player?* He explains further. The actor's father is Black and mother is Hawaiian. This actor impressively "specializes in writing and dramatizing Hawaiian myths and legends at the Bishop Museum, dances hula, speaks Hawaiian." But now, he writes, the actor "is exploring his 'Black side.' He happens to be openly gay, so that might further enable him to make such decisions."

I'm incredulous. Scare-quoting "Black side" strikes me as especially unbelievable. And now he has dragged his cis male view of queerness into the equation too.

This white man's confused racial analysis has gone so completely sideways, I have to finally admit I have nothing left to say. I'm totally exhausted trying to convince this gatekeeper that a critical conversation about systemic racism and decolonizing multiraciality might be of value to Hawai'i. Self-care is key in this work, and I decide to save my strength for a fight I might actually win. I never write him back.

And my book never does visit the islands.

"The wonderful diversity of books, ideas and music," his email signature reads, "that defines us."

Five months following, 45 is elected and the neo-Nazi vampires rise from their coffins. He's your President too.

Aloha. Mahalo.

ALOHA

An earlier version of this chapter originally appeared on my former blog, Multiracial Asian Families, in June 2015.

A year before this "Aloha" email, I went to the movie theater to see a white-made rom-com by the same name. It was a hot June afternoon in Seattle, and, I recall, I was supremely annoyed then too.

I was annoyed because *Aloha* the movie, set in Hawai'i, had just come out and a white woman had been cast as a Mixed-Race Hawaiian Chinese Swedish character. I was annoyed because it was sunny outside but I was stuck inside a stale theater that smelled of too much popcorn and fake butter because I was an active blogger on multiracial issues and felt I had to weigh in. But most of all, I was supremely annoyed at Asian Americans for the way the whole thing was being talked about.

A passion project of white director Cameron Crowe, *Aloha* is the story of a dejected white military man who "finds himself" against the backdrop of tropical heaven by betraying and rebuilding the trust of Native Hawaiian people and falling in love with a military-serving Hawaiian Mixed woman. Despite Crowe professing admiration for Hawai'i, allegedly researching in-depth and building inroads with real-life Native Hawaiians, the movie still ended up entirely white-serving and white-centered, replete with a central white cast, People of Color appearing only as supporting actors, and the genius move of casting white actress Emma Stone as the Mixed-Race love interest.

Still, it's rare that any sort of portrayal of Mixed-Race Asian people enters public discourse, and I knew that *Aloha*, as a mainstream Hollywood film, had the power to author my story whether I wanted it to or not. So I saw the movie that day because I saw an opportunity to get a glimpse into how society views and thus treats people like me, and to say something about it. And though I squirmed disagreeably in my theater seat for so many reasons, finally I just made my body still and resigned myself to watching.

First observation: *Aloha* was overall a really bad movie. It was surprisingly bland to look at, for a movie shot in an incredibly beautiful place. The acting was subpar and painful. The plot was pointless and uninteresting, boring as hell to sit through. There was nothing basically compelling about the movie at all. After, I would read that even white people didn't like it. White critics gave *Aloha* dismal reviews for lousy directing, a dreadful script, mismatched A-list actors, poor production.

Second observation, and the far more important takeaway: Set in Hawai'i, where Native Hawaiians continue to be besieged by whites and the military, the movie centers white people and the US military anyway, but that's supposedly made better by the conceit of a military-serving Mixed-Race Hawaiian Chinese Swedish character, who is played by a white actress. Roll credits, lights on. Thank you for coming and remember to leave your trash in the receptacle on the way out.

As I gratefully left the theater that day, trying not to dwell on the two hours of my life just lost forever, I knew this second observation would form the core of my written response as a Mixed woman. But when I went home and read some more, preparing to offer my voice into the conversation about how miserably the film had failed, I uncovered something that made me far more lastingly vexed than those two hours in that theater seat ever could.

Asian American reviewers nailed with complete clarity that casting a white woman in the role of Mixed-Race Woman of Color was crap; that blatant Hollywood whitewashing against a Hawaiian back-drop merely renews the license on an insidious practice that keeps marginalizing People of Color. However, as their scathing critiques kept rolling in, here's what I really started noticing: "Why is Emma Asian," "Emma Stone Isn't Asian," "Not Buying Emma Stone As an Asian-American," "Asian Emma Stone." I read these reviews by Asian American brothers and sisters, feeling ill at ease, increasingly skeptical and frustrated, then enraged and infuriated.

Aloha is a film set in Hawai'i that, yes, doesn't depict the many Asians who live there, but ultimately the setting is a place that has been stolen from the Native Hawaiian people. Yet in the conversation led by my sisters and brothers, that crucial point seemed to be getting subsumed under the shadow of their politi-cized Asian America. Even multiraciality seemed to be less interesting to Asian Americans than the fact that Emma Stone's character was supposed to be a quarter

Chinese (read: Asian). This narrow framework set a trend for all racial criticism of the film:

> [Multiracial people] comprise the fastest-growing population in America. Which makes Crowe's choice of Stone as the melanin-free embodiment of Hawaiian soul and one of the most prominent part-Asian characters ever to appear in a mainstream Hollywood film so baffling.
> — *Entertainment Weekly*

> Emma Stone, a white actress best known for her role as a white savior with a heart of gold in "The Help," plays a character who is ostensibly the result of an Asian penis interacting with a white vagina.
> — *The Frisky*

> *Aloha* actually features one of the more prominent Asian/mixed heritage female leads in any studio movie in recent memory. She just happens to be played by Emma Stone.
> — *The Daily Beast*

> In an industry that already severely lacks Asian representation on the big screen, they get EMMA STONE to play an Asian … Have you learned nothing from *Breakfast at Tiffany's*? It's offensive. And it's offensive to let the talents of many Asian actors go to waste. Plus, it's just plain rude pulling this during Asian Pacific American Heritage Month.
> — *Complex*

Of all major reviewers who attempted an anti-racist analysis of *Aloha*, as far as I could tell, none were of Native Hawaiian descent, less than half were of mixed descent, and not one objected to the character's *Hawaiian* identity being represented by a white actress. It was as if, for them, a character being Mixed and Asian completely eclipsed her being Indigenous. Which just seemed plain wrong to me. But I wasn't entirely sure. I called my fierce Native Hawaiian friend, scholar and activist Maile Arvin, to get her view. Maile was unsurprised by the whitewashing of *Aloha*:

> Hollywood doesn't usually do well by Hawaiians. The tourism industry depends on all these movies about white romance in Hawaii. It's not lucrative for Hollywood or tourism to tell any other story. There are so many movies that are shot in Hawaii and often they're not identified as [being in] Hawaii, like *Lost* or *Jurassic Park*. Hawaii is often used as the backdrop for all these stories that are about uninhabited islands— or if it's about Hawaii, it's about white people falling in love.

Maile said she'd heard the movie-makers were claiming, in their defense, that Cameron Crowe loves, adores, and respects Hawaii; that he researched his film for months and worked to incorporate the story of the Hawaiian people. But, she added:

> I'm not really interested in what they think is a more culturally competent movie but

still is a white romance. It's fundamentally flawed. It's about a military contract and using Hawaii to protect the US from China and Japan … I haven't seen critique of that. I've seen a lot of critique of the word "Aloha" [but] more fundamentally it's a settler/colonial movie. It's not just about the name of it but the story they tell about Hawaii.

What Maile said she'd been far more interested to see was so many articles by People of Color criticizing *Aloha*'s whitewashing when, by contrast, *Descendants* (which also featured a Mixed-Race Hawaiian character played by a white actor, George Clooney) drew so little attention in 2011:

It seems like the Emma Stone character being Asian has sparked more critique than *Descendants*. Nobody seemed to have a problem with George Clooney playing a Hawaiian. [So] for a large audience, Hawaiians looking white isn't a problem, but a Mixed Asian person looking white is unbelievable. Which is kind of disturbing. The wider public thinks that Hawaiians could look like Emma Stone, but if they're mixed with Asian, they can't. It seems connected to larger problems like the API [Asian Pacific Islander] designation and Asian Americans speaking on behalf or over Pacific Islanders. It shows gaps in solidarity.

In the end, she shared with me the kind of intention and action it really takes to build coalitions and work in alliance with the Native Hawaiian community:

> There are definitely a lot of mixed families and people who are Asian and Hawaiian. They are not necessarily always in conflict. At the same time, a lot of people who aren't mixed [Hawaiian] grew up on the island and identify as Hawaiian. That's the same problem. It just covers up Native Hawaiians again. And Native Hawaiians are erased from so many things. It's important to be clear about how you represent yourself. For example, there are some Asian American activists [in Hawaii] that identify themselves as Asian settlers. Some people hate that idea. But it's a way to express solidarity and really involve in activism with Native Hawaiians.

At which point everything coalesced for me under her leadership.

I wrote my blog response to *Aloha* and included the gift of Maile's words and brilliance. I wrote that I was deeply invested in exploring the facets of a Mixed-Race Asian identity in a raced/racist world, but not a conversation about that identity that moves toward anti-indigeneity. I was starting to understand such sliding as a form of racial wedging, where Asian Mixed identities are used to further divide People of Color's solidarity in service of advancing white supremacy. I cautioned readers that we needed to be far more aware about the ways we were critiquing *Aloha*, admitting that I was maybe even less concerned with Cameron Crowe and his dumb movie than I was worried about our narrow analyses working to reify the oppression of others.

And I asked:

If Asian Americans are outraged by Hollywood whitewashing because it erases us—do we do much better when we erase Native Hawaiians ourselves?

CHAPTER THREE

Food

When exactly this coconut-water craze started on the continent, I'm not entirely sure. It was confusing when the sleek drink boxes began appearing on expensive store shelves, and tuneful promises about the newest health fad played in my oversaturated ears. I assumed coconut water would taste like the sweet coconut drinks I sipped as a child in Asian markets in America and Asia. But it isn't. It's not sweet. Is this a thing? It's a thing. So I start buying too…

Now it's 2017 and we're going back to Hawai'i soon. Well, my husband and I are going *back*. It will be my son's first trip. For all of us, it will be the first time visiting the islands with friends who have "local" ties.

On O'ahu we will visit with my Korean girlfriend, her Korean Japanese Okinawan husband, and their two children. He grew up in Hawai'i, the descendant of plantation workers and activists. My son calls him "Uncle."

On Kaua'i we'll visit with a white friend who lived on the island for a long time as a young woman; it's where she gave birth to her only child, also an Asian Mixed boy, the same age as my son.

The trip will be a unique opportunity to dig deeper into our identity as an Asian Mixed family. Nevertheless, the complex questions I had previously asked about Mixed Race identity and Hawai'i have, for the moment, faded behind the sheen of my present-day excitement. But also my nervousness. *Nervous why?* I don't want to be a tourist but I am a tourist. And that might be okay if I weren't holding too all this Hawai'i-belonging I get assigned that I can't live up to, and the way not-be-longing there loudly amplifies all the not-belonging of my existence. Because of what Hawai'i represents for Asian Mixed people like me, so much of my mixedness can't help but project, play, and replay in stereo through this one short trip.

We're brainstorming things to do with my Korean girlfriend and her husband. "There's a Target, if you need anything," my Korean girlfriend suggests. *Wait, what?* Thinking how I was planning to go to Target here in Seattle tomorrow to look for masks and snorkels, but maybe I shouldn't bother.

"Dave & Buster's!" she adds. Flashback to when I went to Dave & Buster's in San Diego. Not my favorite place. Lights, noise, greasy food, college kids, money evaporating into cheap games that spit out paper tickets that get you even cheaper toys.

"What kind of food do you like?" asks Uncle. I freeze. *Umm. Crap. That's dumb. Why can't I remember.*

Food. Always the damn food. It's not meant as a pop quiz, but it feels like one. One that I'm going to bomb. When you're Mixed Race, so many things feel like tests. Some of them aren't. Then again, a lot of them are. And a lot of them are designed exactly for you to fail. Which is why this food question has me on prickly pins and needles, and my tongue is tangled in neural circuitry misfire.

"Where do you eat out in Seattle?" Uncle reframes the question, noting my hesitation. I'm still frozen. *Shit. I don't know. Think, think, think.*

"Uh, we eat pho a lot," I at last answer haltingly. "And, uh, we eat at that Hawaiian restaurant down the street."

Uncle smiles. "That's not real Hawaiian food."

Fuck. Failed.

"Do you like poke?" he follows.

I don't say anything. It's so embarrassing admitting I'm not the world's most adventurous eater. I struggle with seafood, I don't do raw fish. Read: she doesn't eat ethnic. Read: she's not really ethnic. *But my mother is a white woman.* I'm having this stupid humiliating argument in my head, I feel ashamed, should I say? Shouldn't I say?

Finally, "No, I don't eat poke." *Fail again.* I glance to the side. I fidget in my seat. Uncle nods once. Smiles again. Thinks to himself. Honestly, he's probably just pondering other fun things we can eat. But in my head I've decided he's thinking what an inauthentic asshole my palate is.

There's some mention of eating real Hawaiian food and then, surprisingly, a cuisine I recognize and love. "We should go to Chinatown." *Chinese food!* I relax. This is the food of my ancestors. "But the Chinese food in Hawai'i is so different." I tense again. "Different" from what—*Chinese* Chinese food? I feel bewildered by this statement, given that my taste for Chinese food comes from childhood trips spent in Taiwan with my Taiwanese family. Does this suggest that in a Hawaiian context … I'm too authentic?

Hold on. Did I fail this test or not?

Head explodes.

Then, a bizarre turn.

"We like to eat from the deli at Whole Foods," admits my girlfriend. I'm reminded of how my husband and I subsisted off the deli at Seattle's PCC (Whole Foods competitor) when we were remodeling our home, but the food was so expensive it almost broke our already tipping bank. Also, how that PCC recently closed and a new, mammoth version just opened its doors down the road, ushering a light-speed jump in the gentrification that's pushing People of Color out of our south-end Seattle neighborhood.

Whole Foods just opened their newest store on Oʻahu this year. It's the fourth store in Hawaiʻi. On our trip, we will shop at this new Whole Foods. Once. Like all Whole Foods, it professes proud support of local farms and producers. But I won't understand when I see the inflated prices on its floor, compared to the incredibly low prices of Asian and Pacific Islander farmers at local farmers' markets out in the community.

Whole Foods: a Texas-based natural-foods chain with hundreds of locations nationwide. "The store," a news story explains about the Oʻahu location, "is positioned between two planned ultra-luxury condominium projects—Anaha and Waiea—being developed by The Howard Hughes Corp." Howard Hughes Corporation: a major real-estate development and management company, also based in Texas. "It's awesome for Whole Foods, awesome for Hawaii and awesome for our team," the store team leader says. The Whole Foods CEO and cofounder is an anti-union white man. The Howard

Hughes Corp. CEO is another white man, who built his first condo when he was a teenager.

I think I get it now.

We will end up going to Whole Foods on O'ahu with our friends, even though Uncle's parents raised him on Foodland. I'll get the impression Foodland must be a bad store. Poorly stocked, dingy and dirty, low-quality foods. Or something. I don't know it, so I assume.

Meanwhile, I do know Whole Foods as a "main-lander." I know it very well. Especially coming from Seattle, which has an obsessive white food-purist culture all its own. So I'll go to the O'ahu Whole Foods knowing what to expect and, just like on the continent, I'll be wholly horrified by the high prices, the blatant food elitism. I'm very familiar with who shops at these stores, who they're meant for and not meant for. I know my immigrant mother-in-law, who grew up impover-ished in post–World War II Japan, would never shop here because it would seem unfathomably excessive. I know my immigrant Taiwanese father, who was never poor, still wouldn't shop here because the food wouldn't make sense to him and the prices would seem outra-geous and stupidly American.

On Kaua'i, no longer with our "local" Asian friends, it'll be me and my husband and our son. We'll need to shop on that island too and will try to decide between the two nearest options: Safeway or Foodland? Safeway we know—again, because we also have it in Seattle. Where I live, it's the chain grocer you're likely to find in poorer, Browner, Blacker neighborhoods. The products are okay, the prices not as low as they should be, the lines long and slow. Our instinct is to autopilot to Safeway because it's familiar. But also because, remember, in my head I'll have this dingy, dusty, dirty image of Foodland. Last minute I catch myself. Uncle's parents shopped Foodland.

"You know what, let's try something different," I'll suggest. "Let's go to Foodland."

Once inside the Kapaʻa Foodland, my husband will exclaim, "This is actually a pretty nice store!" It'll be surprisingly nice. Clean, organized, well stocked. Way better than Safeway. And we'll discover Foodland is not only a locally owned supermarket chain in Hawaiʻi, but helmed by a Mixed Race woman. The store was founded in 1948 through a partnership between an Asian and Pacific Islander woman affectionately known as Momma Lau and an Irish immigrant to the islands. The Irish immigrant ended up marrying one of Momma Lau's daughters, and his own Mixed daughter has served as Foodland's president and CEO since 1998.

We will eventually figure out, however, that farmers' markets are where residents mostly shop on Kauaʻi because the cost of food is too inflated otherwise. Adds up when we pull into the parking lot of the Kalāheo farmers' market. That time there'll be only a couple of vendors, two older Asian and Pacific Islander women who remind me of my ama and my son's obaachan. "You're late," one of the women will scold, which I'll accept because I grew up around the unbridled scolding of elder Asian women and it feels entirely familiar. The women sell out of the backs of their cars. Papaya, limes, mizuna for mere dollars. "Wait, how much?!" my husband will ask me to repeat, disbelieving but deeply impressed.

Whole Foods, Foodland can't hold a candle to these prices, yet still win consumer and visitor hearts anyway with their big-box stores, big and bigger spaces. The elder women at Kalāheo I would imagine get lost in the fray at times. It takes a while for me to realize, though, I still haven't fully peeled back the layers to the pit, the heart of things. That is, the 'āina and the food practices of its first peoples, the Kānaka Maoli, which are the most lost of all: on one level, overwritten by settler farmers of color; on another level, constantly suppressed or pushed out to make room for imperial military, tourist, and corporate ventures.

Drive just eight miles north of the Kāne'ohe Foodland on O'ahu, near Uncle's intergenerational home, and you will arrive at the lush Waiāhole and Waikāne valleys. Following the overthrow of the Hawaiian Kingdom, a haole businessman took hundreds of acres in these valleys, becoming one of the top ten land owners at the time. He dug a ditch in Waiāhole and daily siphoned away millions of gallons of water from the valley's traditional kalo (taro) fields to the dry plains of central O'ahu's thirsty sugar plantations.

Kalo, first child of Papa (Earth Mother) and Wākea (Sky Father), is the elder sibling of Kānaka Maoli, and as such, its cultivation is a practice of not just sustenance but also deep spirituality for Native Hawaiians. Amputating water from Waiāhole's kalo fields is thus tantamount to dismembering Kanaka from their family and collective wellspring. Waiāhole kalo farmers have fought this hostile intrusion for decades, growing a taro-roots movement as part of the Hawaiian Renaissance, and galvanizing community support to rally behind their water struggle. They are still there, and the struggle continues.

As long as I can remember, living on the continent, I've been buying a certain kind of cheap, low-shelf white sugar from Safeway. C&H Sugar, in those pink-and-white paper bags, the logo enclosed in a navy-blue circle adorned with a tiny pink hibiscus. It hasn't ever occurred to me to consider what the "C&H" stands for, but I mention it to my Mixed husband now and his eyes grow distant with a sudden old memory. He looks down, gathering together this recollection, hums a little, then unexpectedly sings out a jingle: "C&H pure cane sugar, that's the one!"

He looks up, surprised at himself, shakes his head, laughing. "Hawai'i, C&H Sugar, isn't that a thing?" he asks. I have no idea what he's talking about. "I remember that song from commercials when I was a kid," he recalls, explaining to the confusion written across my face. My husband watched a lot of TV growing up in the 1970s and 1980s. "Look it up," he tells me, now very certain about these C&H commercials. I better see them. "It's a thing."

C&H: California & Hawaiian Sugar Company. The vintage commercials aren't hard to find on YouTube, where they've been archived lovingly by unknown users. Multiple ads cast with Mixed Asian and Pacific Islander actors, children and adults, who look exactly like me and my husband and son. *In Hawai'i, our children grow up with the sugarcane! Pure cane sugar from Hawai'i, grown in the sun! Island sugar growing pure, fresh, and clean!*" That catchy jingle, which embedded itself so deeply into the psyche of my husband's childhood brain that he can still sing it word for word.

When the white man first came to Hawai'i, sugarcane was already growing. It had been introduced by Polynesian voyagers, the first people on the islands, who had arrived millennia earlier. The white man began to grow it on his own, quickly strong-arming his plantations into a big-business oligarchy (upon the back of cheap imported Asian labor) that dominated Hawai'i's economy through land alienation, marginalization, and disenfranchisement of Native Hawaiian people.

C&H was founded in northern California in 1906 and imported raw sugarcane from Hawai'i for decades to be refined and sold on the continent. Beginning in the 1960s through the '80s, when my husband and I were children and when the Sovereignty Movement was on the rise, C&H commercials regularly aired on television depicting Hawaiian children happily chewing sugarcane and dancing hula to the iconic C&H jingle. Nowadays, the California and Hawaiian Sugar Company no longer sources from Hawai'i, as the islands' plantation industry has declined and the global sugar market has changed. C&H is more likely to source internationally from Vietnam or Brazil and locally from Louisiana, Florida—

And from Texas. Home base of Whole Foods and Hughes Corporation.

Full circle.

I'm making my way through the interlaced and knotted strata.

Whole Foods.

Which, as I write, has just been bought out by Amazon. The mega-retailer wastes no time dropping prices. A month after returning from Hawaiʻi, I'll read the headlines.

"Amazon is the new Walmart—and Whole Foods just inherited all of the e-commerce giant's baggage."

"Amazon is trying to destroy supermarket retailers."

I'll read more. "Shares of Kroger, Wal-Mart, Target, Costco, Supervalu and Sprouts Farmers Markets collapsed Thursday after Amazon said Whole Foods will cut prices."

I'll think about the lofty promise the Oʻahu Whole Foods made to stand by resident farmers, and I'll think that seems pretty unlikely if multibillion-dollar grocers like Kroger, Walmart, and Costco are collapsing under the gargantuan weight of Amazon, which, ironically, is headquartered where I live. And never mind the Kānaka Maoli, I suppose, who have been forgotten entirely.

The arrival of the haole to Hawai'i brought a distinct entrepreneurial view of the land. The Hawaiian significance of places was hidden behind haole technology and architecture. Resort, military, industrial, residential, and highway development ravages our 'āina. Man has replaced the gods. Man has forgotten their names.

— KAPULANI LANDGRAF,
"Ai Pōhaku," in Asian Settler Colonialism: From Local Governance to the Habits of Everyday Life in Hawai'i, *Candace Fujikane and Jonathan Y. Okamura, eds. (2008)*

Happy talk, keep talkin' happy talk
Talk about things you like to do
You got to have a dream
If you don't have a dream
How you gonna have a dream come true?

— "HAPPY TALK,"
by Richard Rodgers and Oscar Hammerstein II,
South Pacific *(1949)*

CHAPTER FOUR

First Gear

YWCA Kokokahi is perched on eleven acres of waterfront property. There used to be a long pier where people could fish or dive, but it has fallen into decay. Across the water Moku o Lo'e, known as Coconut Island, rests serenely. In the 1960s the opening sequence for Gilligan's Island was filmed here. "The first mate, and his Skipper too, will do their very best to make the others comfortable in their tropic island nest." Moku o Lo'e originally belonged to Hawaiian ali'i (rulers), and traditional life there consisted mainly of fishing and farming. But it was overtaken by haole men, the US Navy, and a Japanese real-estate investor, and now it's completely owned by the state...

I finally call the car-rental place in Honolulu. Friend of a friend of a friend works there. *"Here's the bottom line price, call them!!"* texts my Korean girlfriend. *"Tell them you were referred."* She knows, I assume. She's married to a "local," has family there, goes to Hawai'i every year. She's trying to help.

My first excuse was that I had a cold and lost my voice for a few days. Which I did. But it was still an excuse. My next excuse was doubt. *"I don't know,"* I hesitated, asking my friend, *"Will they be able to offer a better price than I found online?"* She was confused. Of course "local," and someone you know, is going to offer the best price. *Right. Of course.*

Tsk, tsk, Sharon. Excuses, excuses. I finally call. I use all the reference names.

"Hi, my name is Sharon. Um. I'm coming to Oʻahu. I need to rent a car. And, um, I know somebody that knows somebody that knows you. So, help me out?"

The guy on the other end is unimpressed.

"Oh, okay," he returns flatly. "Let me look and see what we have." I muse over whether or not this man is Asian. That's how I see him in my mind. Maybe he's even Mixed, which is likely, given around one out of four people on the islands identifies as Mixed Race. I don't know. But I do know he can't see me, and without this body (maybe even with it?), without my "local" friends by my side, I have no cred in what I've been told is this hybridized dreamworld. I'm just another tourist to him.

They're sold out of compact cars. He clicks at his computer, does his job methodically, robotically, looking up the next level of pricing. He's not very nice or friendly. He gives me a quote. It's more expensive than what I found online. He's entirely uninterested.

"Ummm, all right," I stumble awkwardly, embarrassed. Then, slowly, "I guess I'll just look around a little more and call back if this is what I'm going to do."

"Okay," he answers again, still unmoved. He doesn't care. We end our call.

I text my friend immediately: *"Called car rental place. More expensive than what I found online."*

She writes back, *"Damn! Hawaiʻi is insane, so not ok!"*

We text a little more about tourism in Hawaiʻi and how "locals" hate it; how public services are neglected because so much money gets funneled into catering to tourists.

But I'm a tourist.

We're here.

As my son and I disembark in Honolulu, the airplane's white captain, standing by the cockpit, meets our eyes jovially and says, "Welcome back!"

An Asian woman greeting passengers as we step onto the jetway looks us over and says, "Welcome home!" Hands clasped before her, colorful lei adorning her neck, she smiles warmly.

I can't stop giggling.

Home.

We grab our bags from luggage claim and head outside, where we wait too long for the rental-car shuttle. There's a big crowd. Everybody's waiting and impatient. It's cramped, hot, humid. After a very early and long flight, my son is tired, hungry, and increasingly cranky by the minute. I start snapping at him because I'm tired, hungry, and increasingly cranky too. Shuttle upon shuttle arrives, leaves. I crank my neck to see into the street, looking for our ride. My body gets stiff and painful from standing and stress.

After almost a half hour, the shuttle finally arrives. The driver is a large Brown man in a terrible mood. He doesn't smile, doesn't make eye contact, slings luggage into the back, motions passengers to get in, irritated. Once inside the shuttle I see he's so large and tall that he barely fits into the driver seat. His head is crammed against the roof of the vehicle and he has to stick one long leg out to the side to make room for the other leg to drive. He doesn't, or can't, clip on the seatbelt.

Then the driver glances in the rearview mirror and sees a surfboard leaning precariously against the luggage rack. It belongs to a slender, blue-eyed blond white man sitting in the far back with an arm around a Brown woman, presumably his wife, and two Mixed children at his side. The white man is tan and athletic, good-looking in a catalogue kind of way. Likely, I imagine, he knows what he's doing with that surfboard. But still, I reflect, there's something about his cool surfer-dad image, in stylish, crisp swimwear, that makes his Brown Mixed family look like trophy accessories. I feel uncomfortable.

"I told you to move that board," the driver growls at the white man. But the white man won't accept being scolded like a child in front of everyone and so meets the driver's gaze, pissed off: "I *did*."

The driver rises from his seat, tall, looming, and turns around to face the white man, who looks almost petite by comparison. The two men's eyes lock, get smaller, flare. Masculinity is rising to a fever pitch in this already hot shuttle.

"No," levels the driver, his voice tight. "You didn't." Chin raised, the driver looks down at this white man like he hates him, even though they clearly don't know each other at all. Slowly, stormily, the driver gives a final warning: "I *told* you to put it over there."

But the white man's not giving in. He raises his chin too, defiant. And he raises his voice. "I don't know what you're talking about," the white man insults. "You're not making any sense."

That's it. The driver's fury is unleashed. His face becomes mighty and ferocious, his Brown body seems to grow even larger still, and I can feel every passenger in the shuttle quickly suck in and hold their breath. "I TOLD YOU TO MOVE THAT BOARD," bellows the driver powerfully, not yelling exactly, but in a low, loud voice that feels like it's using all the last breathable air. "MOVE IT NOW."

The white man won't cower, you can see it in his face. He's not scared. But at the cooing, prompting, and caressing of his Brown wife, he finally gives in and moves the board silently. She just wants it to stop. The white man purses his lips and settles back into his passenger seat, ticked off, while the driver, shaking his head, vexed, pushes himself back into the driver seat where there isn't enough room. The white man's Brown wife half smiles, consoles her husband, "Okay! Everything's good. We're on vacation, in Hawai'i! Woo-hoo." She's not looking at anyone else, but she's speaking to the rest of us too. There's a bright flower tucked behind one of her ears under her long hair.

I'm pretty sure if these two men had been alone on a beach somewhere, they would have fought. But they're not. We're in a Honolulu airport shuttle, driven by the Brown man, that's taking the white man and his Mixed family, and me and my son, to our tropical vacations.

On any given day in Hawai'i there are hundreds of thousands of visitors. Last year alone, a shocking 9.3 million tourists came to the islands and spent over $16.8 billion. The majority of visitors come from the US continent and Japan, with an increasing number from mainland China and Korea. Most of them visit O'ahu. *Like us.* It seems to me that residents' hands, settler and especially Native, must be tightly tied here in an economy so clearly dependent on tourism. *Am I a fiber in that rope?* The numbers are growing, and it's unclear what can be done or if anything will be done at all.

A handsome young man is working the counter at the car-rental lot. Although undeniably Brown, now he's the one with bright-blue eyes and light hair. *Mixed*, I can't help but assess instantly. When it's our turn, I see him scan me and my son also, registering a similar conclusion. *Mixed.* Does something click, lift, shift? It feels like there is recognition between all three of us. The young man is extra friendly, extra polite, extra kind; walks us outside and sends us helpfully on our way. Yet another warm welcome is comforting and allows the shuttle conflict to be forgotten momentarily. *I could pretend I belong here.*

But then I drive the rental car, a Fiat, in first gear all day, thinking the transmission is fucked up. Heads turn at the sound of the ailing engine laboring down every street. I feel eyes on us everywhere. My face warms. *Haole. Tourist.* Now I probably fucked up the transmission myself.

In Native Hawaiian genealogy, Papahānaumoku, or Papa, the land, is mother. Native Hawaiians are descendants of Papa (Earth Mother) and Wākea (Sky Father), who created the Hawaiian islands. Kānaka Maoli are thus inseparable from the 'āina, and they care for Papa with love and respect, knowing they will also return to her one day. The Kingdom of Hawai'i was strong and vibrant for millennia until interference by colonizers cracked the earth with disease, land theft, and dominance.

This origin story has never been allowed to make its way to me, Asian Mixed girl on the continent, even as the image of bodies like mine have long been used by both "mainland" and "local" narratives to obfuscate the truth of what's being done still to Hawaiʻi's first people. Mixed kids in white spaces, my husband knew "Hawaiian War Chant" and the C&H Sugar jingle, my sister knew *Blue Hawaiʻi*, I knew *South Pacific*. It makes my stomach churn how insidious it was, to us and others, that we were taught to know ourselves only as complicit through such grotesque, oppressive fairytales.

But even when we went to Hawaiʻi, was there ever any revelation in that? Like the earth's soil packed below the paved city streets, Hawaiʻi's truth is buried and suffocated beneath layers of tourism, overdevelopment, militarism, and a settler culture taken over by Asians.

Hidden

in plain sight.

Here are the things I remember:

I visited Hawaiʻi for the first time with my family as a preadolescent, Oʻahu and Maui, in 1989. I would've been eleven years old. I went again as a teenager, to the Big Island. If memory serves. I think there might've been even more trips. My white mother got the Kamaʻaina discount in stores because of her Brown Mixed daughters. She was confused at first why the prices were cheaper at the register than labeled, but she was mostly just glad to pay less.

My memories from those early Hawaiʻi visits are scant at this point, for a midlife-approaching woman pushing forty. Memories get foggy, hazy, dreamy. *Did that really happen or am I telling myself a story about what really happened?* One thing I remember—we always came as tourists. My parents traveled staunchly as tourists everywhere we went: staying mostly in hotels, never straying off the beaten path, signing us up for tours led by well-rehearsed travel guides, hitting all the tourist hot spots and digesting local culture only as neatly packaged for visitors. There was never any intention otherwise.

I remember standing, my feet buried in the caress of soft sand, on a Maui beach at sunset. My family was there too, but they faded to unimportant. The wind was blowing warm breath, the palm trees were shifting into silhouette, mother ocean was stretched out before me, her waves rolling, stretching, reaching over and over to comfort the shore. There was a peace in me that I had rarely known at that point and have rarely known since. It was so magical to me then, still magical to me now, and I doubt I'll ever forget or stop being grateful to Hawai'i for this gift.

I remember we stayed in a condo on Maui, and there was a sticky mousetrap in the bedroom I shared with my sister. A small mouse had been caught. Trapped and petrified, he didn't move, though still alive. I wanted to save him. I pulled him gently from the trap and tried to wash off his sticky fur in the bathroom sink, which didn't work. Eventually I gave up, placed him on the balcony, and closed the glass door, hoping he would run away, that he would make it. But he was so exposed there and just as trapped. I was young and didn't think it through. I kept worrying and peeked out onto the balcony minutes later. The little mouse was gone. But there were birds and birds and birds circling overhead, and in my heart, I never believed he made it.

I remember Honolulu, some hotel. As I recall, the room was too small for our four-person family, but my parents, who had plenty of money, often made peculiar attempts at frugality because their wealth gave them anxiety. I slept on the balcony because I felt claustrophobic inside the room. At night, sex workers strode the sidewalks below, looking, waiting for work. Someone told me Japanese businessman were often their customers. But I don't remember thinking or caring much about that.

What I do remember is that sleeping on that balcony, up high over the city and the sex workers, in the warm night air, sounds humming around me, was one of the best memories of my childhood. I'm not sure why. I remember so much in sharp detail. I remember being alone. I remember being happy. I remember being away from my family. I remember loving the warm air and knowing the ocean was nearby. I slept well. I woke at ease. What a trivial thing, maybe, but it was so reassuring sleeping on that second-rate hotel-room balcony in Honolulu.

I remember liking Waikīkī, the bright water and the hot, bright sun. Years later, my husband and I had a layover in Honolulu long enough to make a dash for Waikīkī. He'd never been to the islands. *Let's go real quick and take a dip. It's so pretty.* I couldn't believe it. There were more bodies stuffed onto that beach than seemed humanly possible. Piles and piles of tourist flesh, tubby tummies and burnt skin, muscled frat boys in backward caps and waifish bikini babes in belly chains. Across the street was unrecognizable. Built up bougie so high and so wide, stacked and packed with high-end hotels and restaurants and shops. It oozed money, class, someone else's vacation, callous frivolity. It was disgusting. I was disappointed for my husband. That this was his first experience. I never wanted to come back again.

I remember the new resort on the Big Island with the train that ran through it. You never needed to leave, because everything you could want was right there. I think they had dolphins to swim with. There were multiple pools, each fitted with its own slides, rock formations, deck chairs, and bars for the grownups. If you did leave, which you probably wouldn't, there was just more shopping, golf courses, and resorts for miles. The Big Island's stunning natural black-sand beaches were an afterthought to that resort experience.

I remember Kaua'i with my husband. The first time for fun. We were so busy, so young, so thin, so full of energy. We had some money to play with then. Rented a convertible and drove around shamelessly like the tourists we were. Hanalei. Queen's Bath. Princeville. *So rich.* Kapa'a. South Shore. Po'ipū. Waimea. Red dirt, salty seas, suntans, snorkeling.

We went to a luau because it seemed like something you were supposed to do. My parents had taken me multiple times as a child tourist. *You should go just once. It's kitschy but fun.* We chose a local Hawaiian family-owned luau. "The best on the island," brochures boasted. It was everything you'd expect. Brown people in grass skirts, leis, and not much else. Photo ops with good-looking young Pacific Islander women. Lots of hula and Hawaiian food. A pig roasted in a pit. Visitors a sea of white, pasty faces, baseball caps, collared shirts, and khaki. We were self-conscious because we knew we stood out and because the consumption of culture by tourists felt hard.

While we ate, elders of the Hawaiian family that owned the luau roamed the large dining room, greeting guests. I remember music, singing, an ukulele being played upon a small stage. The matriarch of the family, a Brown grandmother with white-gray hair in a sunny Hawaiian dress, moved across the floor like a goddess, captivating everyone. I watched along adoringly. She turned, met my eye, smiled wide and made her way toward me. "You look like you belong to the islands," she said warmly, pausing at my side. My heart burst with joy. But then the grandmother moved away, joy melted into the silent white stares of the other guests at our table, and I felt stupid, confused, strange.

The second time we went to Kaua'i, we got married on a beach in the surf. We stayed in a little yellow house across the street from the ocean. A vacation rental. It was cute and quaint. One night a young Pacific Islander woman knocked at the door. My husband answered, spoke with her gently. She was in distress and needed help. But there was nothing we could, or would, do for her in that moment. It strikes me now what that represented. We were staying, as I recall, in a neighborhood where "locals" lived because we wanted less of a tourist experience. But when the actual life of Brown people on the island punctured our illusion for a flash, we were frozen by our ignorance.

Here are the things I never knew:

When I was born an Asian Mixed baby in 1970s Hartford, Connecticut, to my white mother and Taiwanese immigrant father, Native Hawaiian resistance to US occupation was resurging in Hawai'i. Launched by Kalama Valley Indigenous residents protesting condemnation of their land for residential and commercial development, the Hawaiian Movement (later, the Hawaiian Sovereignty Movement) grew as a collective of political struggles and grassroots initiatives. The decade following was characterized largely by anti-eviction struggles and land claims.

By the time I was taken on my first trip to Hawai'i, in the 1980s as a child tourist, the Movement had evolved into a larger struggle for Native Hawaiian autonomy connected with Native American activism on the continent. Government abuse of lands that were supposed to go to Kānaka Maoli had been challenged by multiple demonstrations, occupations, and lawsuits, and Ka Lāhui Hawai'i, the largest sovereignty initiative in Hawai'i, was founded.

When I went back with my family as a teenage tourist in the 1990s, radical feminist Indigenous-rights activist and professor Haunani-Kay Trask released the first edition of her seminal book *From a Native Daughter: Colonialism and Sovereignty in Hawai'i*; the Peoples' International Tribunal found the US guilty of genocide against Kānaka Maoli people; and Ka Lāhui was creating the most comprehensive plan yet devised for the attainment of Hawaiian sovereignty.

When I visited Hawai'i two more times with my husband shortly after the turn of the millennium, twelve thousand Kānaka and allies had just taken to the streets of Waikīkī, marching down Kalākaua Avenue in red Kū i ka Pono shirts, a sea of crimson. Meanwhile, Hawaiian-language revitalization was making incredible strides. The first master's degree in a Hawaiian studies field had just been awarded, and the first doctoral dissertation written in the Hawaiian language had just been completed.

Another decade and I've returned again. This time as a political writer, photographer, and activist; also woke woman, wife to an Asian Mixed man, and mother to my own Asian Mixed child. But do I comprehend any more than I knew before?

I remember a waterfall. Where was that place? There were peacocks. There was a show where an unnamed Pacific Islander, wearing traditional garb, did a dramatic high dive off the top of the falls. Then all the tourists got to swim in the pool below. So cheesy. Even as a non-woke teenager I found the high dive performative and cheapened. But the pool was peaceful and happy.

I ask about visiting a waterfall again this time. I think my son would love it. But Uncle hesitates. He advises it's really not a good idea. Leptospirosis. We could hike to one, but we really shouldn't swim. Uncle was raised to be very careful about leptospirosis, so I take his advice seriously. Later, on Kaua'i, I'll ask my white friend the same, about visiting a waterfall. She also hesitates, notes waterfalls are kind of a hike, which might be challenging with my son, and there are also a lot of mosquitoes.

"Oh," I accept, defeated. Then, to make it okay, "And anyway, Uncle told us there's some disease we should be careful of, right?"

"Leptospirosis?" she asks immediately. My friend pauses, half smiling through a corner of her mouth. "Yeah, you don't really need to worry about leptospirosis that much," she explains knowingly, pragmatically. Not a big deal to her at all. "It's not as contagious as it's made out to be."

I feel puzzled and upside down. All these different ideas, tellings, ways of seeing the same things, just work together to keep it all out of focus and frustratingly unclear. But anyway. We never do go to a waterfall.

HAOLE

An earlier version of this chapter originally appeared on my former blog, Multiracial Asian Families, in February 2015.

> [She] never told the son who was crippled by polio about her relationship with his father. All she said was that the man was an American, a sergeant in the Army. He was one of the thousands of GIs who left children behind as victims of the conflict that the United States never officially called a war.
>
> — IRENE VIRAG,
> *"Life and Times of Le Van Minh"*

A half decade back I was producing a lot of writings on white-mixing not being synonymous with whiteness, particularly regarding Asian and white children and people like myself. Some of my pieces: "Why Mixed with White Isn't White," "Are Mixed Race Asian/ Whites, 'Basically White'?" and "Talking Mixed Race Identity with Young Children," in which I described my Asian Mixed son asking if he were white or Black at four years old, me telling him he was neither, and him bursting into tears. Then there was my first book, an officious research project, which provided ample evidence of the subtle to overt racism Asian Mixed children were facing.

Sometimes I received vitriolic pushback: "You know damn well that you benefit from 'White privilege'." "You and the baby daddy are clearly white." "You just need to calm the f down … stop over analyzing." "Stop confusing the poor child … Have some decency as a parent."

It was the voices of a few, yet a sentiment I realized I was seeing reflected everywhere. I knew, put together, the comments represented a larger social cynicism and distrust of people like me and my family that was very real.

Many people still view Asian and white Mixed bodies as "pretty much white" or "the next whites" and therefore white-complicit hench(wo)men immune from racism, even the villains topping society's racist organization. As physical embodiments of the racial hierarchy's two top-positioned groups, we often face a tremendous amount of resentment that disregards our diasporic histories, testimonials, and lived lives. Because we are light-appearing mixes with close white family members and near generational ties to whiteness, it is incredibly difficult for communities of color to imagine us People of Color, and much easier to envision us as honorary inductees into the world of white privilege. If we are "light" and "half-white," then we must be "basically white." Initiate mass write-off.

The blotting out was enraging
and I had more fire then.
So I pushed back at the pushback.

There are a lot of problems, I argued, with the idea that Mixed Race Asian-and-white people are simply white. One, the idea disallows space for contemporary Asian-and-white people to discuss the racialized experiences we *do* have when we are viewed as nonwhite. Two, the idea that we are "basically white" ignores that the oppressions we face stem from a long transnational history of colonization, war, and migration integral to the larger race conversation. And finally, the idea that we are "basically white" diverts from a crucial point that it is not Asian-and-white Mixed Race people who created white supremacy and the systemic racism we struggle to undo.

Racism targeting Mixed Race Asian-and-white people has deep significance that gets dismissed far too easily, I kept arguing. Recall, for instance, that miscegenation has historically been illegal expressly because Mixed Race children would dangerously dilute white purity, undermining the racial order and threatening white supremacy. It was Mixed Race children of partial white descent who were of especial concern and viewed as the grossest aberration. Any white-mixed child or adult, then, occupies a particularly contested place, capturing the attention of the dominant group because our bodies encroach upon the borders of whiteness. This place becomes a stage upon which aggressive strategies of dominance can get played out with notable exaggeration.

I could prove it.

Case in point, I said: when the first Chinese male laborers came to America, they could fraternize with Women of Color without much consequence, but they were strictly forbidden to fraternize with white women, centrally because of the children they might produce. This racism that loathed the possibility of Asian-and-white Mixed children was sharply exemplified in 1892, when famous English (white) social scientist Herbert Spencer wrote:

> "I have ... entirely approved of the regulations which have been established in America for restraining Chinese immigration ... If the Chinese are allowed to settle extensively in America, they must either, if they remain unmixed, form a subject race standing in the position, if not of slaves, yet of a class approaching slaves, or if they mix they must form a bad hybrid."
>
> — *from Proceedings of the Asiatic Exclusion League*

American GIs (predominantly white), I added, have left in their wake huge populations of abandoned Amerasian children following US military presence in many Asian countries, including Vietnam, Korea, and the Philippines. These Amerasian children have often been not only excluded from American citizenship and orphaned by their fathers, but then treated horribly in Asia as unwanted reminders of US dominance. Yet even in the US, during World War II internment (1942–1946), Mixed Race Asian Americans of Japanese descent were interned if they were as little as one sixteenth Japanese.

I kept pushing back.

Even if Mixed Race Asian and white people are seen as some sort of loaded "good hybrid," this has still not

84

typically freed them from being racialized, oppressed, and yet again diminished. Rather, their "interesting" bodies under the microscope can become an even more convenient target of discriminatory beliefs.

For example, Hong Kong prostitute Suzie Wong, in the 1960 film *The World of Suzie Wong*, was seen as very beautiful. Suzie was played by Mixed Race Asian and white (Cantonese/English/Scottish) actress Nancy Kwan, who skyrocketed to fame and was sometimes called "the Chinese Brigitte Bardot." But the character Kwan played is also highly criticized as what writer Sumi K. Cho calls "the Hollywood prototype for the masochistic eroticism of Asian Pacific American Women." There is even a scene where Suzie Wong invites her white male love interest to beat her so she can show off her injuries as a measure of his affection. Kwan being Mixed did not at all allow her to be white. In fact, viewers had no trouble imagining her as a racialized other and subjecting her to a demeaning gendered, racist typecast that then served to further the oppression of all Asian Pacific American women.

A final big push.

This was all to say no, I continued—thousands, even millions, of Asian and white Mixed Race people worldwide are not white and have never been treated as such. Further, the othering of Asian and white Mixed Race bodies is an important component in constructing race as it has been socially upheld for centuries—a construct that engulfs us all.

It's necessary to know these Mixed Race truths, I advised, and also to know the role silencing plays here (because telling me I'm "basically white," and to shut up, does exactly that). Stories of discrimination have been silenced for millennia. Silencing is a major way in which the hierarchy remains intact and injustice prevails. One of our greatest struggles, then, in undoing racism is learning how to receive the stories of others nonpredatorily and with true attempts at understanding. That means as we struggle to hear and honor the stories of people marginalized by this construct, we should always avoid telling anyone their oppression is unreal or untrue.

Remember, I wrapped up, the practice of silencing is what oppressors have done for practically ever. Let's not use the oppressors' tools to keep oppressing. There are many stories within the story of race, and they all matter. We can't ever know the whole picture if we aren't willing to see its many component parts. And if we can't see the whole picture, it will be near impossible to make things better.

Exit with a flourish and flush of adrenaline.

That's how I did it.

At least,

in those days.

Time has taught me something I didn't realize at first, when I was certain I could go on forever sizzling with rage. Pushing back is hard, hard work. The louder you get, the more intense the pressure to stay quiet becomes.

Recently I was contracted to facilitate a Mixed Race affinity group for staff and faculty at a Seattle public school. The white and People of Color groups had already started. A Mixed Race group had been added later, after much back and forth about whether or not it was worth it. When I finally showed up for my first day, multiple bags and my tired son in tow, no one at the school knew I was coming.

I stood there confounded. An African American woman at the front desk called in a white staff member, and the two attempted to piece out the puzzle of me-and-where-I-was-supposed-to-be for at least fifteen minutes. As a Mixed Race–identifying person who often finds herself in racial limbo, the whole fiasco seemed so perfectly symbolic I couldn't help chuckling to myself.

In the end it wasn't funny at all. After figuring out nothing, the white woman plunked down guiltily beside me on the sofa where I had sat to rest and issued a helpless "I'm so sorry." At which point the African American woman at the front desk, clearly fed up with wasting time on me, muttered loud enough for us to hear, "Maybe she just belongs in the white group." All humor vanished, replaced instead by the special kind of hurt that comes when other People of Color deny you. The white woman next to me shrank a little, glanced over worriedly, but kept her lips tightly closed.

I quietly packed up my things and left.

Then, there was the big TV station that decided to tape a series of parent conversations on race. Each of the conversations represented a single-raced group (Black, Latinx, Asian Pacific Islander, white) talking about the tough topic over a staged dinner. There was a call to the community for parents willing to join the Asian Pacific Islander taping, and my name was recommended. After some careful research, I agreed to participate but made a point to underscore for the recruiting party, an Asian woman, that I was multiracial. The response was swift.

The spots had already been filled but anyway,

"We're going with full Asian this time."

And there was the time I agreed to do an interview for a local Asian publication on growing up interracial. I was worried because we, the children of miscegenation, are so often reduced by whites and monoracial People of Color to either hybrid heroes with superhuman racial powers, or the tragically downtrodden, doomed to wander the earth lost, depressed, and eternally confused. We are rarely seen as whole people, filled in spirit, full in our nuanced humanity precisely because of our complexities. Still, I wanted to support my community and the article's writer. So I went forward.

When the article came out, the writer never let me know, though she had promised to. It was poorly written and she had not practiced due diligence, interviewing only two people of Asian-and-white descent and neglecting to represent anyone who was Brown. The piece, framed around tragic confusion, was titled "Identity Crisis: The Unique Challenges of Mixed Race Children." My brilliant Black Filipinx friend told me she hated it. On social media, another Black woman I didn't know disdainfully commented there was no such thing as Mixed Race and if I educated myself properly I wouldn't have such "mixed snowflake identity crises." There was fallout and in-group fighting, other Mixed people were hurt, and I felt like it was all my fault.

I used to get so mad when people like me were quiet on the subject of our mixedness. But I understand now why silence sometimes seems the easier choice. Keeping those multiple antagonizing forces at bay, trying to stand your ground as it jolts beneath you, to continue speaking your truth as others put their fingers in their ears—it will make you exhausted in a way you never imagined. No one can go on like that forever.

And as your mental and physical stamina start to give way, it becomes harder and harder not to let their truth become yours.

CHAPTER FIVE

Brown

The sky is scattered with palm trees and coconut palms that are, I find out, almost all non-native to the islands. They're exotic. Which makes me chuckle. It's the words "native" and "exotic," sure. But also, I know this game. Just like in Los Angeles, where I grew up: they're an iconic symbol of the place, yet not of the place at all. Sweet stories, tourist trappings, postcard perfect. "Actually," my friend tells me, "the Pacific Islanders brought the trees as a resource when they came, a long time ago." That makes sense. I nod. It feels better. Where are coconut palms native, though? None of us knows...

There's a call for a new anthology: Asian American women on their experiences of colorism. The editor is calling for Mixed Race women too, which is awesome. I'm kind of excited and think maybe I should submit. But have I had experiences of colorism, oppression based on the relative lightness or darkness of my skin compared to other Asian Mixed women? And then the uneasy thought—I don't know if I have. *But I'm not white.* And again, for the gazillionth time since I started this work, the walls come crumbling down around me. I shouldn't be writing about race and racism if I'm white. *But I'm not white.* I'm taking up too much space. *But*

I'm not white. How could I ever offer anything into this work that's worthwhile? *But I'm not white.*

Before we left for the islands I was standing on an old towel one evening, hair flipped over, looking at the bathroom floor, lost in a labyrinth of unexceptional thinking. My eyes suddenly snapped into focus. The towel under my feet was bright pink with white flowers and "Hawai'i" scribbled in white letters again and again across its fabric. *Where did this towel come from?* I couldn't recall. Probably Target.

I was touching up my grays with black brown, brown black. I have never liked my natural hair color. I started dyeing it away as a teenager way before I was woke, before I knew I'd do what I do now. Then, it was jet black, blondes, reds, and pinks. Short, shorter, then spiky. I hated my natural Mixed hair color, a color I often see on Biracial Asian white people. To me it was a mousy, shitty brown. Boring, crappy. Different. In between everybody else's brown hair. Not dark enough to be Asian and yet still strangely different from the brown hair that grows from the crowns of white heads. I got rid of it as soon as I could.

I still dye my hair, but it's different. I've become more self-conscious of how Asian I look than I've ever been. Partially it's because racial-justice organizing is coalesced behind politicized racial identities of color. But I'm a light-skinned Biracial Asian woman and there's no politicized racial identity for that. Only tepid multiracial fiction that's whimsical and spineless. Dark hair, I surmise, makes me look more Asian, or at least more ethnic. I think. So I work to pull it out. I can at least be an Asian American, or a light-skinned Woman of Color. I don't want to risk looking white (my husband says I never could anyway), and I guess I can't just look like myself.

You would think showing up for undoing-racism work would have also allowed me to come into my own power. But clearly in some ways it hasn't at all, and my loneliness has only deepened. For instance, in the process of admittedly internalizing my own oppression, my eyesight has become grossly affected. I've lost the ability to see other Asian Mixed people like myself. How many times have my husband and I watched a movie, seen someone walk by, and he could nail it right away but I had no idea, when I used to be able to nail it too…

"She's totally Mixed."

"Wait, she is?"

"What, you didn't notice?"

"I had no idea. I thought she was full."

"Whoa. Are you serious?! That's pretty disturbing."

Another example. Whenever I spot elder Asian Americans who've gone gray or white strolling the city streets, I've decided they all look less Asian when their dark hair changes. But I don't think that's actually true. Which I then find super upsetting, especially as I myself am getting grayer by the year. And I'm sad to see that something has regressed in me—that what I'm seeing is being misperceived through a damaged filter fraught with litmus tests of belonging, not belonging, passing, not passing, being, not being, and self-hate.

Then again, recently I cut my finger with a kitchen knife and couldn't dye my hair for a while. My lighter gray and natural medium-brown hair had grown in about an inch when the comments began coming in too. First, I was wearing a bun out one afternoon when I said to my husband that I thought it made me look more Asian, and an elder Japanese woman stopped me with, "I don't think you look oriental at all." About a week later, I was paired with a Chinese American woman at a training, discussing prejudice we had faced, when she leaned in to say, "Well, at least you got the good genes—you don't look foreign at all." Then, about a week after that, my son was examining a picture of me as a child when he suddenly observed, "No offense, Mom, but you looked Asian as a kid and you don't really look Asian now."

As soon as my finger was well enough, I immediately dyed my hair dark brown, almost black, again. Within days, the Cambodian landscapers who help us maintain our yard stopped me while they were working because they had to ask, "Are you Cambodian?" They were mesmerized, intrigued, because they thought I looked like them and perhaps hoped to claim, rather than deny, me. *I'm never going to stop dyeing my hair again,* I heard my inner self say. I couldn't help it.

It doesn't feel good to confess any of this. It feels foul and disgusting. Shameful. Making matters stupidly worse, the number of self-righteous feminist articles I've had the displeasure of scanning that attach a woman's power to her willingness to let grays grow in. I wonder if the women who write these self-congratulatory pieces started going gray in their twenties, like I did. I wonder if those women have white eyebrow hairs that frost across plucked fields of brown. I wonder if any of them are Mixed Race, Biracial, particularly "mixed with white." I've had brief moments where I've tried—where I'm like *Fuck yeah, I'm going to let it grow in.* Then I think about the consequences and I'm like, *Naaaaah.* Sigh. *Guess I failed that test too.*

Sometimes I lean into the bathroom mirror, consider instead the small spots that have, midlife, begun to appear across my cheekbones and the bridge of my nose. People of Color tend to find these spots cute, resulting in a lot of comment about me being "Asian with freckles." But dermatologists, all white men, warn me the spots are from too much sun and from getting older. I better wear sunscreen every day, they threaten, and stay in the shade. They offer to get rid of the spots with expensive laser treatments that are only 50 percent effective. I leave their offices feeling like a deformed, hybrid freak.

I've seen many Asian women, here in the US and overseas in Taiwan, China, Hong Kong, and Japan, who carry umbrellas on sunny days and cover up as much as possible. I don't know if they're worried about skin cancer. But I do know they're worried about protecting their ivory complexions (those who have them), which are considered a mark of high beauty and class. I also know that women who have been born with brown skin in these places will always struggle to be seen as glorious.

At Ala Moana Beach Park, white-skinned brides from Japan materialize seemingly every thirty minutes to take wedding photos on the beach with their young Japanese grooms. This beach, like Magic Island next to it and Waikīkī down the road, are completely man-made, which I find so unbelievable I'm not sure what to say. In Seattle we have a handful of small man-made beaches because we wouldn't have beach otherwise. *But why do you need to make a beach in Hawai'i?*

Kālia is the ancient name for this place. It was once a swampland with fishponds, where many Kānaka fishermen worked and lived. In the early 1900s, Hawaiian families were displaced by haole developers, and the swampland was filled in with sand to create a park for tourists and beachgoers. It was renamed Ala Moana, "path to the sea."

A century down the road, ghostlike Japanese brides form an endless parade across Ala Moana's imported sand. It's humid and hot, but their dresses are perfect and crisp, and the women don't seem to sweat. Flowers are arranged flawlessly in their updos; not a hair moves in the small breeze. I'm astounded how pale these brides are, their skin like milk. *How can you be that pale in Hawai'i?* I realize they must stay inside, in the shade, under umbrellas and away from beaches while they're here. They come to the sand, perhaps, only for these pictures. I watch them pose, impeccably styled and pale against the sunny backdrop of the islands. They're smiling and they must be happy, yet the photos of their happiness are forged and fraudulent. I don't get it.

An hour passes. My girlfriend will admire resident beachgoers, by contrast: "They're so good-looking here." We'll be sitting in the sand, watching. It'll be hard not to agree. It's island culture. "Locals" are brown. Young. Attractive. Stylish. On a different day, driving to a beach, we will see a man, a resident, at the side of the road. Shirtless, barefoot, very tan, fit, slender. Also young. But something won't be right. He's jerking, tweaking, dancing, yelling.

"Cracked out on crystal meth, probably," my girl-friend will say. "I would lock your doors."

I'll think if he wasn't high he'd be good-looking too. His eyes are wide and wild. He's saying something.

"Don't make eye contact," my girlfriend will warn.

"It's just me and these two," I tell the Brown woman at park admissions, pointing to my son and my Korean girlfriend's son. "Seven fifty," she replies through the window. I nod, rummage for my cash. She pauses, looks at me again, glances at the kiddos. Hesitates. "Are you a Hawai'i resident?" I shake my head and smile again. "Okay." She understands.

When we go to Hanauma Bay it's still beautiful, but not like how I remembered from when I was a kid. Less beautiful. Less peaceful. Fewer fish. The fish that remain seem enormously stressed by the presence of so many tourists. The water is hazy. I didn't recollect the tiered entry, where visitors aren't allowed in until they've watched an educational video warning them not to kill the reef and harm the animals; nor the parking lot that closes when full, at which point workers turn away everyone else. I thought I remembered tourists parking all up and down the roadside. But not this time.

It's because that stuff is all new. That's why I didn't remember it.

When we meet up with a Native Hawaiian friend who has just moved back to the islands after many years in Seattle, we eat at a longstanding O'ahu fixture, Ono Hawaiian Foods. It's closing in a month after fifty-seven years in business, which residents find foreboding. Kalua pork, poi, beef watercress soup, kimchi, squid luau.

I eat anything and everything here. I'm so relieved to be away from the careful menus of Seattle, where people get migraines from MSG and turn up their noses if you bake banana bread without organic bananas, but they don't eat dairy or eggs anyway. Fuck. I'm so glad to be away from that.

We talk about Hanauma Bay. I remark that it's not like I remembered from when I was a kid. My Native Hawaiian friend nods knowingly. "It's different, right?" she agrees, her words heavy.

I press because I'm having a hard time vocalizing what I intuit has changed. "Wait, what did you mean when you say it's different?"

My Native Hawaiian friend talks about all the beautiful places where she used to snorkel as a child on the Big Island; how there were so many fish, so many turtles, there was so much reef. Now, she says, over-tourism has destroyed and killed a lot of the reef, and there aren't as many fish, and no turtles. I understand. I understand why my memory doesn't match up. Because it isn't the same. Not because I didn't remember it right.

At Hanauma Bay this time, my Korean girlfriend's son observed to me, under his breath, "There's a lot of tourists here." Then even lower, in a hushed voice, "A lot of Chinese." It's a bad thing. He made the observation, I guessed, because it's what he has overheard Hawai'i residents say, adults, likely including his own family. He confided in me like I would understand. But I didn't reply. How could I? My paternal ancestors are from China, and my father loved coming to Hawai'i as a tourist when I was a kid. *And I'm a tourist.*

Another thing my Korean girlfriend's son says a lot: "That's so haole!" Again, I assume he's parroting Hawai'i residents he's overheard; again, the observation is clearly meant as a bad thing. In this case it's something he will often proclaim loudly and proudly. I get it. It's done on the continent too. But I wonder, as I always wonder, how to navigate this stuff as a "part white" person raised by a white mother.

What is Brown to someone like me?

When I was a young woman growing up in Southern California, I never asked questions about the celebrity-and-beach culture where tanning is trendy. I was pretty brainwashed. I went to school with Hollywood people: producers' and directors' progeny, Goldie Hawn's daughter, Mel Gibson's children, the half siblings of the Kardashians. I would lie on the sand in the sun, like everyone else, and roast. Front, back, flip, flip again. Dip in the ocean. Back to the sand.

The child of a darker-skinned Taiwanese immigrant, under the relentless SoCal sun I settled into a consistent gold-to-toasted-brown all year round. With the suntan and my Mixed features, I was unquestionably ethnic, people could always see it, and there was no doubt in my mind that I was a "half-Asian" girl.

Case in point. Once, someone's white mother, a casting director, combed our high school for potentials. She was casting a Kodak commercial and needed Asian talent. There were just two of us. Me, the Asian Mixed girl, and a classmate, who I suddenly recall was Native Hawaiian. How bizarre that I only recall this about him now (or maybe not bizarre at all). I guess we would've fallen more under the "Asian-looking" category. Anyway, we were passable, or passably perfect. We auditioned for the hell of it. They weren't interested in my Hawaiian classmate, but I got cast for … I didn't know what. They didn't tell me. Until the day of the shoot.

I played a tourist in Chinatown taking pictures of a Lunar New Year celebration. It was weird, artless and awkward, and looking back I know now why I seemed right for the part. The commercial was aired internationally. Part "them," part "us," my ambiguous face held exactly the right appeal for the broadest customer base. I was the best candidate to make them the most money. They paid me well, but I bet they paid themselves much better.

I never really thought, back then, about how the color of my skin as a Mixed woman has special implications. Realization has come with moving to a cloudy state where my skin has become lighter than I ever realized it could and I've noticed my ethnicity comes into question in ways it never used to. "What are you?" a Brown woman asked me once. "Because if you said you were white, I would have believed you." I felt so wounded when the woman said this to me—but also, I started to question myself and my Asian authenticity.

Ultimately I came to understand that "getting tan" is more for white people than anyone else. Because when you're a light-skinned Biracial person who browns under the sun, you're less likely to look tan than you are to look ethnic. The shift is bound to result in others treating you differently as an identifiable Person of Color, which, in turn, significantly impacts the way you see yourself, but then ultimately ends in an unholy mental mess when the tan goes away. I'm pretty sure white folks don't have this problem, generally speaking.

But being in Hawai'i unsettles me on this subject more than ever. I've been told repeatedly by people who've lived on the islands that getting brown, or browner, is a thing here too. The browner the better. The construct feels recognizable even as it's totally different. People of Color wanting to be darker on the islands (to look more Islander, Indigenous, ethnic?) is clearly different from white Southern Californians browning to look Hollywood hot. For me, in this liminal body, there is no clarity. Only aggravating questions remain: As a Biracial Asian girl who grew up in SoCal where she was always Brown, lives in Washington where she's always light, yet looks so ethnic after a few days in Hawai'i sun that "locals" and even sometimes Native Hawaiians claim her—how in hell does all of this work?

It's a damn fucking rabbit hole.

If I cover up and stay in the shade, am I doing it because white dermatologists put the fear of God in me? Or am I trying to pass? If I say *screw it* and let myself get brown, crispy, freckled, and more wrinkled, am I doing it to look Hollywood-hot like I was taught growing up? Or am I doing it to look more ethnic, like a "local"? For a multiracial woman, is being brown a costume or a credential, a liability or a passport? How do I get out from under this vexing albatross of narratives about my Mixed racialized body that dictate what's right or not-right about how I look and make it so that any choice I make can't be my own?

So now, watching my Mixed son under the sun in Hawai'i for the first time, I naturally contemplate what he's taking away from this place. To a degree, simple visibility does matter for us. Seeing so many more Asians, Pacific Islanders, Mixed folk; so many fewer white people; but even fewer Black people. But then, in the only place where we look like we belong when we don't belong in the slightest, I ponder where we truly fall on the spectrum of it all.

"It was fun finding geckos with my friend," my son tells me.

My ocean boy. He'd live in the sea if he could. He loves the waves best. We tell him to get out and he wriggles away, runs back in. Sometimes I threaten him with a consequence if he doesn't get out. *It's time to go.* Then he stands dripping wet, his tiptoes just touching the water, watching the waves break. Wave after wave after wave. The stillest I've ever seen him wide awake. Thinking, watching. He turns around with a big grin. *That's my boy.*

He is the brownest of all of us. Everyone else is burning but him. I don't know how he's so brown. "Look at how brown he is!" exclaims my girlfriend. Says Uncle, "He's got good melanin." *The browner the better* (does that apply to Black folks too?). So I'm proud my son is browning. I exult along with everyone else, happy. But then thorny and guilty beneath the surface. My son isn't really Brown, is he? In Seattle he's a light-skinned Biracial boy. So here he's not Brown, he's just tan. But then again, if we lived here he'd always be that brown. Browner.

But also I see the sun spots on Uncle's face, on the faces of other residents. I'm the one who perched a baseball cap willfully on my head and slathered prescription-strength sunscreen on my face to stop the procession of small freckles, exactly because those white dermatologists put the fear of God in me. I ask my Korean girlfriend if residents wear sunscreen. She says they're starting to. I ask if island kids, who are far browner than my boy, wear sunscreen? She doesn't know, but she sounds doubtful.

I look up which states have the highest rates of skin cancer, thinking Hawai'i must be one of them. I laugh out loud. The CDC tells me the highest rates of melanoma occur among white people and in the cloudiest states like Oregon, Vermont, and Washington—where white people live. And me. Still laughing.

"Will my brown skin go back?" my son will ask on the second leg of our trip, on Kaua'i.

"What, like you mean the way it was back in Seattle?" I ask.

He nods.

"Yes, it will, tans go away," I reply. Pause. "You don't like your brown skin?"

He shakes his head no. I'm surprised after how much adults have been complimenting him while here, telling him he has "good skin" and "good melanin."

"But I love your brown skin," I protest. "It's beautiful."

Doesn't matter. He doesn't like it. Is it merely because it's a change he's not used to? Maybe because he's getting too much attention for it? Or is it because he doesn't like that it's brown? Hard to say.

On Kaua'i, my white girlfriend overhears my son ask me this question and perks up. She jumps in, tells me her Mixed son said the same thing at first. He didn't want his brown skin either. He wanted white skin like his mama. But, she advises me, she was able to quickly smooth over the situation.

"I told him his skin is actually better than mine"—she indicates her white arm—"because his has more melanin and won't burn in the sun." *Good melanin. More melanin.* She notes self-confidently, "That seemed to really help, because now he's fine."

She relays her story in this moment as if it's the perfect salve for us too. But my girlfriend's son wanted different skin because he wanted to look more like his white mother. It's not the same. My son already looks like us, his Biracial parents, who aren't white and who both brown easily in the sun like he does. It's entirely different. *Can't she see that?* My husband and I listen dutifully to her suggestions, but we stay silent.

From my 'ohana (family), I learned about the life of the old ones: how they fished and planted by the moon; shared all the fruits of their labors, especially their children; danced in great numbers for long hours; and honored the unity of their world in intricate genealogical chants. My mother said Hawaiians had sailed over thousands of miles to make their home in these sacred islands. And they had flourished, until the coming of the haole (whites).

— HAUNANI-KAY TRASK,
From a Native Daughter:
Colonialism and Sovereignty in Hawai'i (1993)

Come with me
While the moon is on the sea
The night is young
And so are we, so are we.

Dreams come true
In blue Hawaii
And mine could all come true
This magic night of nights with you.

— "BLUE HAWAI'I,"
Leo Robin and Ralph Rainer for Waikiki Wedding,
starring Bing Crosby (1937)

CHAPTER SIX

Roots

I'm making eyes at the coconut pudding. I walk away once, twice. Come back. Finally buy. An elder "local" Asian woman is considering doing the same, but she hesitates. She doesn't want the tapioca if it's too sweet. She's asking the vendor, an elder Asian man, "Is the pudding too sweet?" He assures her it is not. She advises him, "You can't put too much sugar." He nods, assures her again that it will taste good. But she doesn't seem convinced. I never see if she buys the pudding or not. Back at the house I eat mine greedily in the kitchen. I love it and spoon some into my son's mouth. He doesn't like it and refuses to eat any more…

My Korean girlfriend is talking to me about a lot of things but I'm not listening very well—or at all, I'm afraid. Honestly, I just want to photograph the flowering plants of the garden she and her husband have taken us to. Perhaps cliché. But these flowers are replete with dazzling oranges, reds, yellows, a look that's completely unknown to me. I'm enraptured, I can't help it. *Tourist.* I don't care. *It's a man-made garden.* I don't care.

Spikes, triangles, curves, and angles. Sometimes their faces lift to the sun and sky, ready to fly. Sometimes they simply stand strong and bright, confident in the place where they're rooted. Other times they rest comfortably and easily in the shade of large, tropical leaves. Either way they look strong. They're happy, healthy, gorgeous. All the while my Korean girlfriend chats amiably away, her words muffled and indistinct to my distracted mind.

These flowers are intentionally from all over the world: Africa, Hawai'i, India, Sri Lanka, Malaysia, Melanesia, the Philippines, and Polynesia. This place, a sculpted botanical dreamland. Ho'omaluhia, it's called. "To make a place of peace and tranquility." An organized, sprawling four hundred acres on O'ahu, built by the United States Army Corps of Engineers in 1982, for flood protection. Designed and diagramed. Delineated and drawn. Open every day but Christmas and New Year's.

As we're heading back toward the cars I see an old, crusty planter mounted to an unremarkable wood pole. Altogether the thing is ugly and random, appearing strangely and suddenly in the middle of this mystical garden. Nothing is growing from the planter, which is empty and forgotten except for a shallow pile of blackened, dead leaves blanketing the bottom inside. Planter and pole are a tired palette of rusted browns and dark grays against the sensational rainbow of the rest of this place.

I can't help it. I pull out my camera, snap an asymmetrical, off-center shot. I'm inspired, I guess, though when I look at the view screen to see the capture I shake my head. *What the fuck, Sharon? That's a terrible and weird picture.* Still. After this trip, when I get home, I'll look through my photos and realize it's one of the best I got from that garden. I'll end up using the photo to do a reading at an arts expo and I'll overlay it with words about the emptiness of my past and the stories I don't know.

A different island clock is ticking now that we're in Hawai'i. My brain, not whirring so much. I'm body sore, jetlagged, disoriented. Different time zone, different place. Hawai'i. O'ahu. Kāne'ohe. In a house built by Uncle's grandfather. "Can you believe this house has been in their family for two generations?" my Korean girlfriend asks. I can't. I'm impressed. I parrot the same to my son when it's just the two of us. *Can you believe it?* My son asks, "What's two generations?" I explain. He says, "Actually it's three generations because of Uncle." Right. Kids.

Truly, it does feel like an honor to be in this house. Uncle's father is an acclaimed Asian American writer out of Hawai'i. The house is home to probably thousands of books, including his own. I walk the rooms, admire other authors' names, let my eyes linger appreciatively on titles. Some of the books line shelves. Others sit in messy towers from the floor, or in short stacks on tables and counters. Wherever they fit. I love it.

"How many times have you been to Hawai'i?" my Korean girlfriend's son asks. He's been here many, many times and he's about to prove it by beating my number.

"Umm," I count out loud, "five to six times including this visit." I'm a little surprised when I think about it. More than I thought. He's a little surprised too, I think.

"I've been here eleven times!" He beams proudly.

I'm genuinely happy for him. I smile. "That's because your family is from here, so that makes sense." He smiles back.

My son objects, "But that doesn't make any sense!"

His brow furrows with what seems to be bewildering math and baffled logic. "If you're only eight years old, how could you come here eleven times?"

I understand where my son's coming from, which I acknowledge, but it also feels crucially important to treasure the family pride of my Korean girlfriend's son. I explain. "No, no, it makes sense. It's because his family's from here and sometimes he visits more than once a year."

Ah. My son nods, understands. "Oh." It's fine. My Korean girlfriend's son glows, family pride shining like the sun. I'm glad.

His intergenerational family history is strong here, his extended family and community ties prolific, profuse, and powerful. I watch my girlfriend, her husband, their children, sink into the ease of their Hawai'i, of belonging, and it's hard not to feel the sharp edges of knowing I don't have that and probably never will. I'm sure I have rich family history too. But I don't know it. I can't talk about it much. No one has passed stories down to me like they have within Uncle's family, as a cultural legacy across many generations in Hawai'i.

I do remember huge family picnics in New England when I was a kid, to celebrate my Slovakian Great Grammy's birthdays. Being introduced to family members, white strangers. *I'm related to you?* Running around with tons of white cousins, second or third or whatever. Never got how that worked. They were all white. I wasn't. And I always felt like I didn't belong, that their story wasn't mine, I was just visiting.

Flipside, I also remember huge Asian family dinners at Chinese restaurants. Large lazy susans moving in slow circles. Not being able to hear very well what anyone was saying. Skeptical at the unfamiliar food being set on the table. *Sea slug? Gross! I will not try that.* The Shirley Temples so sweet and tasty but I always hated the fake cherry. I only understood a few words of Mandarin. Most of what was said was inaudible anyway. The table was too big, the restaurant too noisy. *Still visiting.*

In my dreams I would love to travel the world, to all the places of my family's ancestry. Mine. My husband's. My son's. Japan, Taiwan, China, Germany, French Canada, former Czechoslovakia, England, Virginia, Connecticut. I would love to dig deep into this Mixed Race family identity we hold. What it means for us. What we have lost. What we hold still. I would love to do this before our elders pass on. I would love to bear witness to and document their stories before they're gone. Because how can we know who we are when we don't know where we came from? And how vastly true is this for so many Mixed Race people born out of immigration, migration, colonization, war, enslavement; across languages, nation states, her- and histories, or just stories.

Months after this trip I'll go listen to three Asian American women artists share their compelling work at the Wing Luke Museum of the Asian Pacific American Experience: a Chinese American self-described "restaurant baby" from Jersey, a Filipina American who grew up being cared for by her lola, and an Asian Mixed woman whose grandmother and mother fled China to Hong Kong as refugees in a boat. The three friends will title their event *A Place to Call Home*, and they'll talk about immigration and generations, loss and decay, hope and imaginings, and ghosts. I'll be seriously and profoundly moved. And, unsurprisingly, I'll relate.

Ghosts and home. Too many stories are never told and die with the elders who hold them. I have so many regrets about the questions I never asked my grandparents. But I was young then and I didn't care. People ask me and I want to tell them, I want to tell myself. I just don't know much. I have little to pass on to my son. He is seven, starting to have more and more questions about who he is. I reach into my past and there's nothing to gift to him. I fear he'll feel just as amorphous and empty as I do being a Biracial Asian person, a minuscule minority, in the very white place where we live. He needs his stories. I need my stories.

Being in Hawai'i now gives me this intense desire again, like sitting at the kitchen table on a Sunday morning waiting hungrily, frantically, as someone else makes you breakfast.

If I'm not from here—where am I from?

Important, painful questions. My mind chews thoughtfully. But something tastes too sweet once more. Is it the islands that give me this desire again? Or is it what I'm perceiving as the islands encased, as I am, in this intergenerational Asian family home?

Where are you from?

Asian people are not from the islands either, even within families that have been transplanted on this soil for generations. Here in Hawai'i, despite its being constantly and violently ruptured by settler colonialism, original belonging remains solely for Native Hawaiians even as they are forced to fight constantly to reclaim it. Descending from the 'āina and thus being inextricably intertwined with it—*this* is powerful belonging. I am awed by, and feel deep respect for, the reciprocal love between the land and her Indigenous children.

We belong to our ancestral lands.

But I have been to Asia many times, to the lands of my Taiwanese ancestors, and there is no belonging there for me. Me. Light-skinned. Obviously mixed. Obviously "part-white." Me. The Mixed girl who clearly doesn't know the culture, doesn't know the language, customs, traditions, anything. Who is clearly "American" even though I don't belong to the stolen land of "America" either. Me. Clearly and visibly the daughter of white colonialism; of trespass, violent wars, contested lines, encroachment, and violated lands. Everywhere I turn in this body, this embodiment, there is no consent.

I drift upon the turning currents of a riptide caught between here and there, there and here, them and us, us and them, *but not me.* Either way, I am ever lost within it.

Circling,

circling,

sinking.

I am landless.

Which is a fairly sad thing to be reflecting upon in this tropical wonderland where it's assumed I belong

but can't belong.

Because I belong nowhere.

"And do you guys know *the* most famous hapa in the world?!" Tyra excitedly asks her petite models, standing together in a field of sugarcane. The models stare blankly at their famous show host, shake their heads no, stunned by her fame and still trying to process the word "hapa," which they've never heard before.

"PRESIDENT BARACK OBAMA!" Tyra screams, jumping and cheering, and the girls cheer too because it's the right thing to do.

America's Next Top Model takes its contestants on trips around the world. Cycle thirteen has traveled to Hawai'i, where this particular episode is built around surfing, sugarcane, and most of all, fascination with "hapas." Native Hawaiians appear only infrequently in quick cuts and as frame accessories.

"You guys are standing in the middle of one of the many sugarcane fields here in Hawai'i," explains creative director Jay Manuel. "Once the Hawaiians started growing sugarcane commercially, they realized they needed a larger workforce. So as a result, people from all over the world in different countries immigrated here to get jobs."

Tyra probes, "So what happens when men and women from different places come together?" The models have no idea. "Babies! Lots of babies that are from different cultures. A mix."

"And it's called what…?" Jay prompts.

"*Hapa*," Tyra enunciates carefully and slowly. "Hapa means 'half' in Hawaiian…"

"That's right," Jay affirms, "and for today's photo shoot, you girls are going to get to undergo a transformation and actually have to portray two very different, distinct races."

The girls cheer again because it's the right thing to do.

"So, are we ready to get started in *a lot* of hair and makeup?" Tyra tells her contestants they'll be transformed into Mexican Greek, Tibetan Egyptian,

Moroccan Russian, Native American East Indian, Botswanan Polynesian and Malagasy Japanese.

Light skin is painted hues of brown and black. White girls put on contacts to darken their eyes and wigs to cover their blonde hair. The sole Asian girl, Jennifer An, is put in the darkest blackface of all and her hair is teased into a fake fro. She is the one who is supposed to be Botswanan Polynesian. On set, posing against the backdrop of sugarcane stalks and the humming of harvest machines, Jennifer struggles to embody this fabricated "hapa" persona. The creative team is frustrated. Tyra starts to panic.

Jay Manuel comes to the rescue. "You know, in Botswana music is heard everywhere you go," he encourages. "Just bringing in a little bit of that beat, it'll register on your face." Finally, Jennifer comes alive. Tyra is relieved.

At the judging panel, Jennifer is up first.

"The girls were representing something in Hawai'i called hapa," Tyra explains to her fellow judges. Then to Jennifer, "So ... what hapa were you representing?"

"Botswana and Polynesia," Jennifer replies dutifully.

Her blackface photo appears on the view screen to the judges' left.

The white guest judge doesn't really care and says something flaccid.

Tyra and J. Alexander tell Jennifer she did a good job selling the necklace she was wearing.

Nigel Barker—who is Mixed Race South Asian and white and whose wife, Cristen Barker, is Chinese and white—tells Jennifer she looks "National Geographic" but not like a model.

HAPA

An earlier version of this chapter originally appeared on the now-defunct site AAPI Voices in June 2014.

What does hapa mean?

I finally asked myself this question a while back for a piece I was writing.

The moment was long overdue.

I wasn't the first to ask nor, thankfully, have I been the last. At this point I don't think we can ask the question enough. Hapa was and still is used by a lot of Asian Mixed people everywhere as a trendy racial descriptor. Admittedly, I used it myself for a time because I had nothing else, and frankly, it just sounded cool. But language is powerful; words carry so much meaning, and when I came to political consciousness, after reading and reading the works of others, I was inevitably taken down this road:

I am calling myself this thing, but

what does hapa mean?

One way to know, I supposed, was to look at how the word was being used.

I Googled it.

It's a "Hawaiian word for 'mixed-race,'" said Hapa Kitchen Supper Club on their website, "coined to refer

to people of East Asian and Caucasian backgrounds."
Hapa Sushi Grill & Sake Bar said on a different website
it was "a harmonious blend of Asian and American." It's
a "slang term," proclaimed The Natural Hapa Bamboo
Bundles. Hapa Time Style Inspiration chirped that it's
"just one of the coolest words ever." There was Hapa
Yoga, Hapa Ramen, Hapa Grill, Hapa Cupcakes;
Hinode was selling a "Hapa Blend" of brown and white
rices and Hapa Culture was selling … erasers?

I called my friend Maile again. Hapa with a capital
H (as I was seeing it used on the continent), she said, is
meant "to denote people with Asian and white ancestry."
But, Maile cautioned, the term's Native Hawaiian roots
look quite different:

> Hapa is a Hawaiian language word literally
> meaning "part." Historically it was most
> often used as hapa haole, which referred
> to a Native Hawaiian person who also had
> white ancestry. As other peoples from Asia
> and elsewhere came to Hawai'i, hapa also
> came to refer to Native Hawaiians who also
> had other non-Native Hawaiian ancestry.
> The word began being used in Hawaiian
> language newspapers in the 1830s, and first
> appeared in Hawaiian dictionaries in the
> 1860s.
>
> For Native Hawaiians, hapa is a way to
> claim and recognize those of us with multi-
> racial ancestry as being integrally part of the
> lāhui, or Kānaka Maoli nation. This claiming

is especially important because along with British and American settlement in Hawai'i, there was tremendous depopulation through the introduction of diseases to which Native Hawaiians had no immunity. The population of Hawai'i was between 800,000 and 1 million in 1778. By 1878, there were only around 50,000 Native Hawaiians. On top of depopulation, US science, law, and popular culture began to divide Native Hawaiians into "Pure" and "Part" categories. Hapa identity was one way Native Hawaiians could refuse racial "blood" logics, and insist that we were still growing as a nation, not dying out.

In my mind, I experienced sudden illumination as Maile kindly connected the dots for me, and also somber sinking at the realization that I had myself become an oppressor through irresponsible ignorance.

I turned back to the page.

Let's talk more deeply about this word "hapa," I wrote in my piece.

The hapa of Maile's people, I could now see, stood in stark contrast to a widely commodified version that lumps together Mixed Race Asians and Pacific Islanders and then magically loses the Pacific Islander part. The losing is no accident, I reflected, whether intentional or not. Collective forgetting stems from a long colonial practice that has for centuries sought to erase and remove Indigenous peoples in order to possess their land without contest.

This is all to say that lumping-then-losing Native Hawaiians is an insidious practice that follows in the vein of what's long been happening institutionally. I looked up some numbers. Consider, for example, I pointed out, that reporting Asian and Pacific Islander in combination (API) on the census was federally directed until Congress approved a revision separating "Asian" and "Native Hawaiian or Other Pacific Islander" (NHPI). Before the categories were separated, things looked pretty awesome for Pacific Islanders. According to numbers generated by the US Census in 2002:

> APIs were much more likely than whites to have earned at least a bachelor's degree (average 48 percent API versus 30 percent whites).

> APIs were unemployed at a similar rate to whites (6 percent API versus 5 percent whites).

> Of all API families, 40 percent had annual incomes of $75,000 or more, compared with 35 percent of white families.

But when the data were disaggregated, things were devastatingly different. In their report reviewing the state of NHPIs based on numbers around the turn of the century, Empowering Pacific Islander Communities (EPIC) and Asian Americans Advancing Justice found:

> Only 18 percent of NHPIs have a bachelor's degree, a rate identical to Blacks or African Americans.

From 2007 to 2011, the number of unem-
ployed NHPI increased 123 percent—higher
than any other racial group, to an unemploy-
ment rate of 14 percent.

NHPIs suffer high poverty (15 percent) and
low per-capita income ($19,051).

It would seem pretty obvious, I surmised, that we
are dealing with some strong settler-colonial echoes
out of the past. But given that the first ten pages of my
"hapa" Google search turned up only happy sales pitches
loaded with utopian visions of an Asian-minus-Pacific-
Islander race-blended future (that you can usually eat),
I didn't know that we were getting the picture. I asked
readers to consider the afterword to Kip Fulbeck's
well-known portrait book *Part Asian 100% Hapa*, in
which sociologist Paul Spickard dismissively writes that
while he sympathizes with Hawaiians objecting to the
appropriation of "hapa," language "morphs and moves"
and "is not anyone's property." "Continental Americans,"
Spickard adds snarkily, "might just as well complain
about Hawaiians using 'TV' and 'cell phone.'" Even Kip
Fulbeck himself became defensive when asked about
the same:

I've actually never heard of any controversy
about the word in real life, having lived and
worked in Hawai'i. It's just not an issue
there. People refer to me as "Hapa" or "hapa
haole" and that's that. Any arguments that
do come up occur only in Internet forums
or academia, and those aren't environments

I'm particularly interested in since they're so removed from the real world."

(FROM WEI MING DARIOTIS,
"100% Hapa: An Interview with Kip Fulbeck,"
War Baby / Love Child: Mixed Race Asian
American Art.*)*

In conclusion, I wrapped up, we need to recognize that attempts to erase Native Hawaiians have been happening for a long time, that those attempts persist on purpose, and that using the word "hapa" without having a) any Native Hawaiian ancestry, or b) any awareness of its history and significance, may make us complicit with white-dominant-colonial agendas, which have sought to wipe away and wipe out Indigenous peoples for practically ever. I offered the gift of Maile's words as I had done before. Maile said:

> It is frustrating to me, and many Native Hawaiians, that non-Native Hawaiians now use "hapa" to refer to multiracial people outside of a Hawaiian context. This erases the use of hapa by our own people to keep growing our lāhui … This extraction is also inappropriate and tone-deaf because the Hawaiian language was systematically banned with colonization. Language revitalization efforts are strong now, but the appropriation of Hawaiian words obscures the existence of a thriving Native Hawaiian language and people.

> If you decide to use "hapa" in a non-Native Hawaiian context, I urge you to not rush to explain away the problems with it, but hold them in tension. Examine the many ways living in the United States can make you complicit with settler colonialism. There are no easy solutions to this complicity, but it is important to struggle against it nonetheless.

And yet there were still thorny questions for those of us who are not Native Hawaiian on the continent and, I think, yes, on the islands too: Would we keep claiming ourselves as "hapa," despite protestations? What did that say about us if we did? And what about this whole "mainland" hapa versus "local" hapa thing? Entirely different?

Or … more similar than we'd like to admit?

CHAPTER SEVEN

Paradise

*"MOM!" my son exclaims, pointing. "Are those coconuts!?"
He's still waiting to live out that lullaby, that island fairytale I sang to him. But I'm having a hard time finding the
fruit the way I'd promised. I examine the large, round orbs
lying on the ground, forgotten, lonely with each other, rotting
by the ocean. One might be brown, another yellowish green.
They don't look right. "Yes," I answer, verging on sadness.
"It does look like they're coconuts." My stomach turns a
little. They look gross. My son wants to eat them and doesn't
understand why we can't...*

"A-lo-HA!"

Tourism ruined the shaka for me when I was a
child. We were taking part in one of the many tourist
groups my parents always joined wherever we traveled. The group was predictably showy and fake and,
for me, embarrassing and awkward. Our tour guide,
disproportionately exuberant, stood at the front of
the bus explaining the importance of the aloha spirit
and "hanging loose." With a cheesy grin, he demonstrated the shaking shaka, thumb and pinky extended,
and encouraged us try this "local" tradition ourselves.
Group members clumsily shaped their fingers and
hands, smiling at each other, giddy over the relaxing

vacation they were about to have. I probably tried too, I'm guessing. I don't remember anymore. But I do remember feeling embarrassed, unnatural to the marrow of my bones, and certain in the conviction that none of us really understood anything about aloha or the shaka, nor cared to.

To this day I can't make a shaka without cringing. So I don't. Even returning to Hawai'i. Even though I see residents use it all the time in casual exchange. I imagine it would take many seasons living on the islands to shake off the yoke of flippancy that tourism managed to harness to this seemingly simple hand sign. And, too, I see that a curtain was dropped in that childhood moment, a curtain behind which there is a spirit of the Hawaiian people I was never encouraged to learn from.

Aloha and Welcome to Paradise. Unless You're Homeless. I don't really want to go to Honolulu. Being from one of the fastest-growing, fastest-gentrifying cities in the United States, I'm burnt out and depressed by city, by people, by traffic, by greed and growth, by crowding and homelessness. There's homelessness in Honolulu too. I'm not surprised, given the tourism and high cost of living. It's a pattern that feels all too familiar.

O'ahu, like Seattle, has one of the highest per-capita homeless populations in the nation. Two thirds of Hawai'i homeless live on this island. Hawai'i, like Seattle, had to declare a state of emergency at one point because their homelessness reached crisis levels. This is all tied to the fact that Hawai'i, like Seattle, is one of the most expensive places to live. And on O'ahu, like in Seattle, the most marginalized populations are the ones hit hardest by homelessness. In Seattle, it's Black,

Hispanic or Latinx, American Indian or Alaska Native, and Mixed Race. In Oʻahu, it's Native Hawaiians and Pacific Islanders.

Not long ago you would've seen homelessness on Oʻahu everywhere, tourists not exempted. But tourism is so important to the economy in Hawaiʻi that something had to be done. Presently, like in Seattle, laws in Oʻahu criminalizing the unhoused have driven them off beaten paths into involuntary hiding, and tourists can rest assured their vacations won't be sullied by having to acknowledge the real suffering of those who are from the land to begin with.

My girlfriend mentioned Hawaiian homesteads more than once while we were on Oʻahu. When it came up, her words were weighed down with sadness. I know enough to know any conversation about land and Native peoples is going to be deeply painful. But I was confused about what homesteads were and, being from Seattle, asked from my reference point. *Are they like reservations?* Not really, I was told.

Homesteads have never factored into any picture of Hawaiʻi when I've visited. As a tourist. As a friend of so-called "locals." As a body that looks like it belongs to the islands. In fact, I didn't know anything about Native Hawaiians at all until I became politicized in my thirties. Even then, when I went back after all this time with a consciousness, Indigenous people of the islands were invisible in the spaces where I was moving. Spaces overrun by tourism, militarism, white hippies, and settlers of color.

In 1921, due to the advocacy of Prince Jonah Kūhiō Kalanianaʻole, Congress passed the Hawaiian Homes

Commission Act in an attempt to stabilize a quickly vanishing Native Hawaiian population devastated by colonialism. The law carved out approximately 200,000 acres in trust for homesteading by Kānaka Maoli. But the responsibility for administering the land has been badly abused and mismanaged by government. In the ninety-seven years since the trust was established, half the awarded acreage has been leased to Hawaiian home-steads, but the other half has gone to *non*-Hawaiians. Meanwhile, there are 29,000 increasingly frustrated Hawaiians on a waitlist as thousands of acres lie vacant.

As they are ironically forced to wait for access to lands that are rightfully theirs to steward, Kānaka Maoli suffer the highest rates of poverty and homelessness in Hawaiʻi, where tourism has driven contemporary housing prices exorbitantly high.

One night, on our way into Honolulu for dinner, we drive past low-income housing. My girlfriend, a social worker, immediately looks it up on her phone. I'm driving in a place I'm not accustomed to and only half listening. My friend is reading from the housing's website and from articles and interviews. I hear "curfew." I hear "Pacific Islander." I hear "killings," "shootings," "safer now."

When I hear "affordable housing," it summons to mind a Seattle panel on homelessness I once attended. At the panel, a smart Black man, formerly unhoused, criticized the misleading terminology of "affordable housing." It's not really affordable housing, he blasted, because affordability is relative, and in a rich city like Seattle, "affordable" routinely results in rent that is inac-cessible to the very poor. The kind of housing we should have, said the Black panelist, is "low-income housing" that takes into account the actual incomes of those in the greatest need. I recall too how they didn't let that Black man talk much, and that white people talked a lot more. He was the only Person of Color on the panel, in a city whose general population is majority white but whose homeless population is majority People of Color.

In Hawai'i, on other days, on other drives, we'll also pass by public schools. It's bad. All the buildings are run down. My Korean girlfriend will tell me about the poor education, drugs, violence, low graduation rates. I only need a couple of headlines to tell me the rest. "In Hawai'i, Public Schools Feel a Long Way from Paradise," says the *New York Times*. "Many Families Sacrifice to Put Kids in Private Schools," says Honolulu Civil Beat. Over half of all students attending Hawai'i's public schools are Native Hawaiian and Filipino.

My girlfriend tells me University of Hawai'i is one of the only universities that hires in-house PhDs for professorships, because the school wants to retain Native Hawaiian students. That seems excellent to me. But then she'll add that, regardless, a lot of the professors are still white. It's revealingly true. Haoles comprise less than half of Hawai'i's population but more than half of UH Mānoa's faculty. Meanwhile, Native Hawaiians make up over a quarter of UH Mānoa's student body but only a little over five percent of faculty. The message is, over and over, ever the same and ever clear. Who belongs. Who doesn't. Who sits on the throne. Who sits at its feet.

In Honolulu, my Korean girlfriend convinces me to at least check out the biggest mall in Hawai'i. It's across the street from the beach park with the white Japanese brides. "Where?" I ask. She points. You can't miss it. The building is gargantuan, and there's so much covered parking that Uncle gets lost driving through it. Ala Moana Center was opened in 1959 by a white developer and businessman who is dubiously credited with "transforming the urban landscape of Hawai'i" because he built mass condos, resorts, hotels, residences, and shopping centers.

Won't lie. The Center is gorgeous, from an architectural perspective: pristine, regal, tall. There's a handsome new Japanese food court downstairs that transports me back to inhaling curry in Japanese train stations ages ago. Upstairs, we stroll, and it sparkles. It's glamorous. The children have room to run and play. Sunlight streams through openings and crevices in long, satin-smooth ribbons. It's entrancing.

But it's bloated with whiteness and money and more whiteness: Diesel, Boss, Forever 21, Nordstrom, Victoria's Secret, Tesla. I stop looking because I feel queasy. High-end white supermodels stand larger than life, their photos plastered floor-to-ceiling, their gaunt girlish frames bent at the shoulders, their bellies concave. I recall the many times Hawai'i folk have insisted to me that race is different on the islands because whites are a minority.

It doesn't feel that different.

At the end of the hall I finally see images of some nonwhite models. Mixed women who are ambiguously Brown. "Hapa" women, I am guessing they might generally be called here. *Oh thank God.* I breathe. They're still models (they're still light-skinned) but at least they're not white. Then. I smile. Of course. It's a Hawaiian company. I snap a photo. *One for the album.*

I ask to duck into a Longs Drugs to buy a couple things. Relief. Fuck. A normal drugstore where you get what you need and things are on sale. I grab sunscreen and an earwax-removal kit. My son needs new slippers. "You've got to buy local," my friend instructs, grabbing the Locals brand. Her boys are wearing them. Her husband says he grew up wearing them.

The boys really want to go to the Lego store. We let them, but I can't help shaking my head. Lego. Started in the workshop of a white carpenter from Billund, Denmark, it's one of the biggest toy companies in the world and makes billions in sales annually. As Lego has grown into its contemporary massive moneymaking form, it has been passed down through generations of white men and is at present owned by a grandchild of the founder. According to *Forbes*, this grandchild, now grown, is the richest Dane in the world with a net worth of $21.2 billion.

My son has brought fifteen dollars to Hawai'i that his obaachan gave him. It's his money, and I always tell him he can decide how to use it. He insists that he wants to buy Lego Minifigures.

Sigh. I challenge him a little. "Why buy something you could buy at home? This trip is special. I don't know when or if we'll ever come again. Buy something you can't get at home."

But no, he insists again. His money has to buy him these Minifigures. Stat.

He buys the Minifigures,
and will never play with them.

While the children are at the Lego Store, my girl-friend darts into Rip Curl to check out swimsuits. I follow. "What's Rip Curl?"

"Oh it's a super-popular brand," she explains, riffling through a rack in front of her.

I contemplate the store. It looks rich and white to me. The suits are designed for much younger women. I feel out of place, and I'm wondering why we're in here. I glance up at the photos along the walls.

"They're all white models," I observe.

"Except for that one." My friend points.

I guess. The man has brown skin, and the photo is out of focus so you can't see his face. He could be Brown. He could also be white with a tan. None of the other photos are out of focus.

"Anyway, it's a Cali brand, I think, so maybe that's why…" She trails off, never saying why.

Turns out it's an Australian brand launched in the 1960s by two Ozzie men, pro surfer friends, out of a garage. They look white to me too, though I can't be sure. The savvy duo made a smart change to their business model in the 1970s, transforming the business into a global brand with revenues of more than $400 million a year. After four decades, the founders eventually stepped down but kept a majority stake in the company. I'm guessing they left with a pretty penny or two in their pockets and that retirement isn't looking too difficult from their vantage point.

Another day, we're at Windward Mall, waiting for the farmers' market that's held upstairs in the afternoon. The kids insist on Toys R Us because they want to look at Legos again. Former conglomerate Toys R Us, in business for half a century, was founded by a white American man on the east coast during the postwar baby-boom era. Having become another mass toy merchant, with over 1,500 stores around the world, Toys R Us until recently generated cool billions in sales every year too. In fact, it was not long ago that the white founder and tycoon put his waterfront mansion in the Hamptons on sale for $13.5 million.

On our trip, in the "girls" section of the Hawai'i Toys R Us (still open at the time), white Barbies line the shelves. Mattel, another billion-dollar company, was founded by two white American men in 1945. Barbie was the innovation of one of their wives, a white woman. I loved Barbies as a little girl and had a huge collection, which included some of my white mother's dolls from the very beginning. When I was a little girl they didn't make Barbies of color. Which became a problem.

Now I'm told hopefully (often by parents defending the brand because their little girls of color can't help being obsessed like I was): "There are lots of Barbies of color!" I believe these parents, but honestly, every time I'm in a toy store I don't see the dolls they've told me about. In this Hawai'i Toys R Us I don't see them either, and I'm confused.

"I thought Barbies were diverse now," I remark.

Uncle doesn't say anything and walks away. Turns out there are Barbies of color, but they're tucked away down the aisle. I don't look at them very long, however, because I don't like Barbies anymore and already spent too much time looking at the white ones.

While we're waiting for the market to start upstairs, we go to what my girlfriend describes as an arcade. It's one of those family fun centers, like Dave & Buster's, where the games spit out paper tickets for worthless prizes. They don't sell food in this place, and the prizes include frying pans and woks. We let the boys run around but decide not to bother paying for playtime.

Adjacent, there's a pet store. They're selling purebred English bulldog puppies for $3,000 each. Kept in a large bins with newspaper shreddings, plexiglass walls, and metal lids punctured with air holes, the pups look far too young to be separated from their mama. There is an older puppy for sale in the next bin—a pit bull mix, the store claims. Because he's a mutt, the price tag is much lower: $399. But anyway, he doesn't even look like a pit bull. He's mostly white with black accents, a cute round head, and a snout that protrudes. Handwritten on his sign, in small print, it says "Mixture not guaranteed."

Out comes the story of the two Hawaiian coconuts
old trees that lived next to a brackish well
along the dry coast at Mākea, near the bay
where the ʻōʻio were once as thick as sand.
Not long ago, someone came along and wanted
the nuts from one of the trees and cut it down.
The other tree is still there
but there won't be any more seedlings.
The male flower always blooms first
and after it dies the female flower blooms.
A single tree cannot make love to itself
and without another nearby of its species
there will be no more young trees.

— DANA NAONE HALL,
from her poem "Native Species"

I touch your hands and my arms grow strong
Like a pair of birds that burst with song
My eyes look down at your lovely face
And I hold the world in my embrace.
Younger than springtime are you
Softer than starlight are you
Warmer than winds of June
Are the gentle lips you gave me.
Gayer than laughter are you
Sweeter than music are you
Angel and lover, heaven and earth,
Are you to me.

— "YOUNGER THAN SPRINGTIME,"
(Lieutenant Cable to Liat), Richard Rodgers and
Oscar Hammerstein II, South Pacific *(1949)*

CHAPTER EIGHT

Blazing

"They were like trash to us," says Uncle when we discover the rotting coconuts lying on the beach. He's remembering growing up around coconut palms. The fruit fell to the ground, no one cared. He and his friends would play beside them like they were nothing. And anyway, "Around here everyone has a machete," my white girlfriend tells us on Kaua'i. "If they want a coconut they'll just cut one open and eat it." It's all so plainly normal, uninteresting. I feel disappointed and think my son must feel disappointed too...

It's uncomfortably, sweatily hot. Humid. Or at least it is for me—the Asian Mixed girl acclimated to the cool, dark days of the Pacific Northwest. O'ahu is sweltering by contrast. My feet pad down the hard pavement of the street and I wing my arms occasionally, making a wind to dry the sweat under my shirt.

Uncle leads us across the way, down a gradual incline, then up a steep road where we can see across the many roofs of his childhood neighborhood in Kāne'ohe. We haven't gone that far yet, but our city boys are starting to complain. They're too hot, they're tired, they'd rather be swimming or playing iPad. We parents either ignore, tease, or reprimand.

At last we make our way to the trailhead. This will be

the only hike my son and I go on the entire trip. Uncle is recalling fond memories of the place from his past. We step off hard, steaming pavement onto the crumbly dirt of the trail and begin our ascent, passing a salt-air-faded sign that reads "Friendship Garden."

Entering the cover of the hillside woods provides welcome respite from the heat. Moods shift, faces lift, and the pace picks up a bit. It's a very different type of garden from Ho'omaluhia, which has ample tiered parking, a visitor center, and huge tended lawns. Here there's no parking, no buildings, no grass. Instead, there are dusty paths that wind up the hillside, plantings that are labeled in some places but seem more wild than deliberate.

It's comfortable and comforting to be in a less frequented, less perfect place. And it feels good to move my legs. We pass a pagoda, a gazebo teahouse, a grove of bamboo where people have carved their letters into the slanted slender trunks, snake plants, and handfuls of bright flowers. Occasionally the woods part to give us glimpses of the suburb growing smaller and smaller below.

At last we crest the hill where the forest pulls back completely to an unimpeded, sweeping panorama of Kāne'ohe and the bay, once a major Kānaka fishery of O'ahu, counterpoint to the great Mokauea fisheries on the west side. There's a wind that wipes our brows, blows our hair gently, and cools our warm bodies. Like most outlooks, the bird's-eye view is dreamlike and totally magnificent. We all stand in place, hands on hips, and look out, contemplating the scene from valley to horizon. Kānaka activist, poet, and author Dana Naone

Hall grew up in this valley. She writes:

> In traditional times, often referred to
> as prehistory, Kāneʻohe was one of nine
> ahupuaʻa (a traditional division of land) that
> lined Kāneʻohe Bay. Numerous freshwater
> springs attesting to the presence of Kāne,
> god of the life-giving waters, fed the taro
> patches and nurtured the fisheries of the bay.
> Driving along the Windward Coast, it is still
> possible to see remnants of fishponds, called
> loko iʻa. Kāneʻohe was a complete world for
> Hawaiians and sustained one of the largest
> populations on the island.

By the mid-nineteenth century, most of this land
belonged to a Native Hawaiian queen who, with the
help of a white partner, introduced sugarcane and started
the Kāneʻohe Sugar Company. The queen died shortly
thereafter, however, and the white man purchased the
land from her estate to continue sugar production.
Asian laborers worked the sugarcane, then rice, then
pineapple, until agriculture completely declined and the
region was transitioned to ranch lands.

In the early twentieth century, another white man
purchased some of this ranch land to create an idyllic
multiethnic Christian community. He wanted to
show that all peoples of Hawaiʻi could live together
in harmony. The upper valley was turned into Friendship Garden. The lower valley was turned into a church
camp beside the bay, surrounded by private house lots.
First choice of lots was given to church organizations.
The remainder were sold proportionately to Hawaiʻi's

major ethnic groups (white, Japanese, Chinese, Filipino, Portuguese, Hawaiian), but only to buyers of "high Christian character."

The white man gave his post-racial Eden a Hawaiian name: Kokokahi, "one blood," after a quotation from the Bible:

"God has made of one blood all nations of men."

At the same time, across Kāneʻohe Bay, the US military was stealing hundreds of acres of the Mokapu peninsula, where they would eventually construct an air station. In 1941, this station would be the first attacked by the Japanese, minutes before the bombing of Pearl Harbor. Native Hawaiians had named the peninsula Mokapu, "sacred place," because it was venerable ground upon which the King met with chiefs. Native Hawaiian burial dunes and esteemed fish ponds still exist there, though access is limited and restricted by the military.

Lifting my camera to my face, I peer through the viewfinder. *Click. Click. Click.* I try to capture the vista spread out before us, but it's irritating because a third of any shot is penetrated by the unsightly marine station jutting out into Kāneʻohe Bay. *Click. Click. Click.* I shift uncomfortably. Slap at my neck. I'm being bitten by mosquitoes, I finally notice. My hand and camera drop to my side. The pictures suck anyway.

Mostly all that's left of the Kokokahi tract is this garden and the camp we can see far below, now the YWCA. Of the house lots, only two pre–World War II homes remain. Meanwhile, the water of the bay has become contaminated from overpopulation, over-fishing, over-dumping, over-dredging, etc. But the military station across the way is still alive and well, sitting on its stolen acres, poised for the next war.

My son and I are at our neighborhood Seattle library one day. He's wandered off to pick too many comic books and movies. I'm hopefully but wearily scanning the titles of chapter books, trying to find something, anything, that's racially relevant for our family. To be fair, I usually find something, which is different from the past, when I'd find nothing. But it's still a lot of work, and the books I do find are often mediocre at best.

I keep looking, letting my eyes drift along the rows of printed covers with those bold letters that grab at your attention, and I find something.

A duo that draws me in like magnets, even though I'm not sure what they are at first. My fingers run down two book spines, and I see myself pulling paired titles at a slant out of the stack. I see illustrated photos of a girl, about the same age as my son, who looks exactly like me. She's posing prettily in purple or pink, always feminine in flowers, against the backdrop of what I can immediately see is Hawai'i.

Her name is Nanea Mitchell, and she's the newest American Girl Doll, released less than two weeks after we returned from the islands. These books are part of a trilogy, her story. She is a historical character, a Mixed girl born to a Native Hawaiian mother and white father, who grew up on O'ahu during World War II.

The books focus on the bombing of Pearl Harbor, its aftermath, and how Nanea "embraces her spirit of aloha and deeply held belief in kokua—doing good deeds and giving selflessly—to do her part for the war effort and help restore peace to her beloved Hawaiian home."

Despite the story of Nanea being based on the life of an eighty-one-year-old Hawaiian Mixed woman, the model American Girl casts for marketing is a thirteen-year-old competitive figure skater from Macomb County, Michigan, who dreams of being a movie star and an anesthesiologist. She's certainly a girl of color, but no one notes her actual heritage. American Girl flies the model to Wisconsin for the photo shoots of the three book covers: *Nanea: Growing Up with Aloha; Nanea: Hula for the Home Front; and Nanea: Prints in the Sand. Macomb Now* magazine calls the teen model "A Real Life Doll."

In stores, the 18-inch doll is priced at $115. Along with the doll's debut, American Girl donates funds to veterans and members of the military, and holds a surprise sweepstakes at stores nationwide for the chance to win a getaway to O'ahu.

Pearl Harbor was one of those compulsory stops on the tours my parents booked when we visited the islands. All I remember was a large white monument on the water; you could walk across and peer over its railings into the sea below. Something upsetting was down there, looming, like a desperate whale in too-shallow waters, or a great white preparing to attack. There was a hush of reverent silence among the many tourists who plodded across the monument's ivory-like floor.

I'm sure our guide, or someone, explained all of this to us at some point. But my recollection contains no words. Only strange sights, a solemn quiet, and that eerie shadow spread beneath us.

When he was six, my son shocked me by drawing a picture of Americans at war with the Japanese. On the front of the page there is a giant American flag; heavily armored, smiling American soldiers to the left; and unarmored, mostly dead, frowning Japanese soldiers to the right. One Japanese soldier fires a gun, but it's clearly in vain against the Americans, who hold, between them, six grenades. On the back of the page there are two grids that chart deaths in great detail, like the scoreboard of a sports game. The Japanese are losing.

At such a young age, my son already had intuition about the wars written into his own flesh. These wars, waged by men, where children get caught in the crosshairs.

While my white grandfather was serving in the air force during World War II, my Taiwanese agong was rushing his eldest children to the countryside to keep them safe from American air raids of Japanese-occupied Taiwan. And I teach my son about internment because I know no one else will; because no one taught me until I taught myself; and because if we had been alive then, both my son and husband would have been imprisoned, and I would voluntarily have gone with them.

This trip to Oʻahu, it doesn't even remotely enter my mind to return to the Pearl Harbor monument.

Part this.
Part that.
Part us, part them.
Pick a side
And never win.
Colonizer's baby
Light-skinned
Half breed
Chink
Jap.

Militarism and tourism are like conniving lovers in Hawai'i. Together, they steal and steamroll the land, paving it with gunpowder and glitter. When the military flexes its ego and commemorates its own memory, tourism pauses to praise it, turning the past into altars of worship. When tourism shrouds itself in a sheen of mythical beauty to beguile the deep pockets of visitors, militarism controls and keeps a strong grip as the bewitching lie is woven and spun. Together, they hide behind a mask to cover up their lie—a mask with a face like mine.

Hawai'i is aggressively advertised as a vacation destination using deliberately gendered images—especially the enticing portrait of welcoming "hapa haole" women. Very specifically, women who are Mixed Hawaiian, Asian, and white. Over many decades, bodies like mine, pictured as availably erotic-exotic in bathing suits or grass skirts, have become one of the most prominent reductive images Hawai'i generates in the minds of potential visitors. It's also the stereotype that generates some of the greatest revenues for haole and Asian men who control the military and corporate tourist industry.

I knew this already. I think I've always known it but haven't had the words for it. It's why "mainlanders" who've never lived in Hawai'i think I must have lived there before, or always. It's why old white men in the public-pool hot tub ask me if I'm a flight attendant and want to tell me their secrets about Jimi Hendrix's last concert on US soil before he died. It's why, as a kid, watching the gorgeous France Nuyen in a tropical tide pool doing hula hands to "Happy Talk," I felt shitty and unsettled. It's why I felt even shittier when white people in the same movie started singing, "You've got to be taught to hate and fear," and I knew they were talking about me.

I don't forget the horrifying reality that 45 is residing commander in chief now, in charge of the army, navy, air force, coast guard, and marine corps. A coercive, bigoted white man is yet again deciding where troops get stationed, where ships are sent, and how weapons are used. All military generals and admirals take their orders from the president. As such, 45, like so many haoles before him, wields tremendous power over Hawai'i, which has been molded over many decades into a mainspring of Asia-Pacific US military strategy.

Built on "ceded" and other lands stolen from Native Hawaiians, Hawai'i is one of the most US-militarized places in the world. The military controls about a quarter of the land on O'ahu, tourism is responsible for over 20 percent of Hawai'i's entire economy, and faces like mine are put on like carnival masks to make it all seem like a good time.

Uncle says, "It's like a cancer," and I consider what it means to be part of that cancer.

If you walk through the neighborhood where I live in Seattle, you'll see yard after yard emblazoned with protest signs: "Black Lives Matter," "I Love My Muslim Neighbor," "Women's March," "In This House Science Matters." Signs I was so critical of before I left, because I didn't believe the white folks here truly stood up for these things when push came to shove. But it occurs to me I never once saw one of these signs in a Hawai'i yard. In fact, the signs were so absent I forgot there was such a thing as yard politics. And now I'm not sure this is such a bad thing about Seattle.

Only once, on O'ahu, do I see a pickup truck with a huge decal plastered across its rear window: "DEFEND HAWAII." There's a rifle pictured beneath the words. I ask Uncle and he tells me it's a street-clothing brand. I look it up. It's not just a street-clothing brand. There's a political statement. But it's a mess:

> Hawaii is often referred to as "the melting pot" because our diversity in PEOPLE as well as cultures ... DEFEND HAWAII simply strives to preserve the notion, to DEFEND the Aloha Spirit, the Hawaii way of life ... Our AR-15 Logo is often questioned, but a gun is the strongest symbolized statement for the word DEFEND. The logo is not meant to provoke violence, but rather figuratively suggest protection by the highest means. We're here to plant the proverbial seed, initiate a positive thought process. To Defend Hawaii, is to Defend Aloha.

Melting pot. I've heard that one before. It's what they used to call Los Angeles. It's what they meant when they proudly (and wrongly) touted my Seattle zip code as the most diverse zip code in the nation. It's a proud self-descriptor in Vancouver, BC, too, where I launched my first book—the term used widely despite there being practically no Black people there. It's also considered outdated racial language, because it fuses difference rather than acknowledging it. I think "salad bowl" was something folks were trying instead. A dish comprising many ingredients whose flavors remain distinct. But I never liked that one either.

Always with the damn food.

Also, defending aloha with an assault rifle that doesn't signify violence? I don't know how you do that, exactly. Especially with the AR-15, a favorite of gunmen who carry out mass murders—the same rifle that killed twenty-six mostly children at Sandy Hook, forty-nine clubgoers in Orlando, and seventeen teenagers and teachers in Parkland, Florida. *Is this Hawai'i brand defending themselves or the gun?* Seems painfully avoidant in Hawai'i, especially—a place forcibly annexed by the US government and occupied still by US military and tourist capitalism.

I can see why Uncle didn't bother sharing any of this.

I scroll through the site's online shop. It gets more confusing, more messy, more painful. "Don't Mistake Aloha for Weakness." "INDIGENOUS." "Teach More HIstory." "Defend Hawaii Education." "Native Lands Matter." Pineapples as grenades. Pacific Islanders as soldiers in camo. Seems to me it could work something fierce if they were driving the irony, if they were pushing the statement, if they were calling out white supremacy. But I can't tell if they are or not.

And anyway, I soon discover, the company is a mimicry, not an original. Carbon copy of a brand out of the continent, DEFEND BROOKLYN, or DFBK, which just opened its flagship New York store last year. Their head designer is Black. I scroll the gallery of the

New York grand opening and see many, many more Black faces.

We're eating at Koa Pancake House one morning. I'm so hungry. Loco moco, kalbi beef, fried egg, spam with rice. Stupid, all that food anxiety I had about coming back. If anything, it's like I came to my food home. Meat and more meat. White rice for days. Farmers' markets like what I remember from Taiwan as a kid, strolling the street markets with my ama. Smells so familiar and nostalgic. Starfruit, guava, mango, papaya, coconut pudding, bananas, durian. Here also, Okinawan sweet potato, lumpia, pad thai, tuna jerky.

I'm chewing, munching, blissing out at Koa Pancake House, when the KKK comes up.

The boys have been talking about the Ku Klux Klan among themselves over the last day, unbeknownst to us adults. It's the first time my son has heard about the Klan, and, not really understanding what it is, he's made an inappropriate joke at the table that has shocked the parents. Questions are asked, the kids' discussion of the previous twenty-four hours uncovered, some education kindly delivered.

And now, my son is terrified.

"Would they hurt us?" he asks me anxiously, eyes wide, worried.

"Well, the Klan's main target is Black people," I say. I have to be truthful, though. I made that promise to myself when he was conceived. I admit, "But I don't think they care for folks like us very much either." Then the part I don't say. *The Klan would see us as half-bred abominations sullying the white race.*

"What is death by choking?" he asks next. It's one of the things he learned during the previous day's exchange, but without adults in the conversation to clarify, my son was totally confused by what that meant. I'm not willing to go too far, especially with a child who is already so afraid. But I explain a little. I assure him he's going to be fine.

But he's not so sure. His eyes grow bigger. It's like I can hear his heart racing, he's so upset and so terrified. "I'm sure I'm going to have nightmares tonight," he tells me.

Ho'omaluhia, O'ahu's largest botanical garden. Kailua Park every day, named one of the world's top ten beaches by CNN and "America's Best Beach" by Mr. Beach in 1998. We're in a multiracial Shangri-la, but my son is petrified of the KKK. He's fixated, asks me questions about the terrorist group all afternoon.

I don't expect I'll ever forget that though we make our home in a white-majority state where there are white-supremacist groups, it was on a visit to Hawai'i, alleged post-racial promised land, that my Mixed Race son of color first learned about the KKK and really understood what it meant for him to be not white.

MALIHINI

A portion of this chapter originally appeared in earlier form on my former blog, Multiracial Asian Families, in October 2012.

Malihini.
Newcomer to Hawai'i.
Stranger among the Native Hawaiian people.
Foreigner.

There are many ways my son has already learned, as a Mixed boy, about not-belonging. The issue of language, words, and names is critical beyond compare. In the very first blog post I ever wrote, I told the story of taking him as a preschooler to his white best friend's birthday party. Of six children, my son was the only child of color. Of nine adults, one man and I were the only grownups of color. This other man had a noticeable non-American accent, so I feel fairly confident in writing that English was likely his second language. Other than this observation, I try to make no assumptions here about his heritage.

The man stopped me at one point and asked what my son's name was. "Kazuo," I answered. He was profoundly confused. He tried to repeat it: "Oh, Cosmo. That's cool."

I sighed inwardly.

"Cosmo" is one of the most common mispronunciations of my son's name. My husband and I felt strongly about picking a Japanese name for our child before he was born. His middle and surnames are English. We wanted his Asian heritage to be prominent. Being very aware of the difficulties growing up with a non-English name in this society, we tried to pick a name we presupposed most English speakers would be able to pronounce easily.

To our surprise and deep frustration, "Kazuo" (pronounced KAH-zoo-oh) has confounded one person after another. We both grew up with extensive exposure to Japanese: my husband because his mother is Japanese, and I because my father grew up in Taiwan immediately following the Japanese occupation. The pronunciation of "Kazuo" seemed straightforward. To us. But we realized after the fact that "u-o" doesn't really occur in the English language. Strangers either repeat a name back that's familiar (like Cosmo), stumble and mumble over it trying to quickly find some convenient nickname, or avert their eyes and refuse to even try. And because of the English word "kazoo," English speakers, if they can even say the name at all, frequently default to placing the emphasis on the second syllable (kah-ZOO-oh) which sounds absurd to me and my husband.

I attempted to help the man. "No. It's KAH-zoo-oh." He tried to repeat it, again with no success. As I frequently need to do, I finally offered the spelling: "No, Kazuo. K-A-Z-U-O." The man tried again, this time with limited success. Looking distressed, irritated, and maybe even a little angry, he exclaimed loudly, "Jesus!" We then launched quickly into some stupid conversation about how my son could go by nicknames if he "needed" to. The man offered me several unsolicited suggestions, like "Kaz" or "K." And in some attempt to make him feel better and more comfortable, I also shared my son's English middle name, explaining my son had an easy alternative if he ever wanted it. The man seemed relieved to hear this.

Later in the party, the kids were all sitting around a table waiting to eat cake. The adults stood behind, watching. A loud white woman (whom I had found out minutes prior was an early-childhood research psychologist with a PhD in infant psychology) tried to help my son. "*Cosmo*, you're doing such a good job waiting," she encouraged him. "*Cosmo* needs a piece of cake," she said, turning loudly on the cake-cutter, "*Cosmo's* been waiting so patiently. He needs a piece of cake." Over and over and over she said his name wrong. Every mispronunciation felt like a gut punch to me. A loud voice resounded in my mind: *You need to stop her. Just tap her on the shoulder and tell her, Excuse me, you're saying my son's name wrong.* But, completely intimidated by her volume, the colossal size of her personality, her impressive academic credentials, her overconfident whiteness, and by a large, mostly white audience—I said nothing. And, I might add, none of the other adults in the room who knew how to say my son's name correctly (including the hosts of the party) said anything either. As far as I know, the woman still thinks my son's name is Cosmo.

Three days following, my shame, hurt, and anger surrounding the incident were palpable and continued to grow. I could still see my son sitting there across from me, looking in my eyes, absorbing every word.

And I didn't defend him. I made excuses or didn't say anything at all. I stewed over what he took away from that party. Did he already hate his Japanese name? Did he already feel different? None of the other white kids had non-English names. When he saw his own mother struggling to defend a personal, beautiful choice rooted in family heritage, did it make him want to reject being Asian?

I shared the story with my husband and we were both edgy and volcanic. Why? Because it's not just about a name. It's about so much more. It's about a society that has greeted Asian immigrants with peonage, discrimination, and exclusion laws. It's about a society that still, to this day, expects everyone who lives here should speak English. And unfortunately, yes, it continues to be about race. In my son's Mandarin class at the time, I had just overheard a white mother explain to her Asian Mixed child that the teacher was speaking Chinese and "English is the language we speak in this country." My son's heritage is English, Welsh, French Canadian, German, Slovakian, Taiwanese and Japanese American. Within the walls of our home he is everything, he is gorgeous, and he is perfect.

But at that birthday party he was Asian, different, and certainly not white.

Now, a half decade later on vacation in Hawai'i, my son has become extremely versed in his otherness, as it has been demonstrated to him repeatedly, growing up on the continent. He was mislabeled an English Language Learner by Seattle Public Schools beginning in kindergarten; endured other students saying his Japanese name wrong all of first grade, with no support from his white teacher; is being called "Chinese boy" in second grade by his peers, and sees daily how children like him are rarely represented, or represented as stereotypes, in the books he reads, shows and movies he watches, and video games he plays.

I confess that in my motherly love, I hoped he would find a salve for that hurt, a respite from othering, on his first visit to the islands seeing so many people who look like him. I can see, however, that I made the same mistake that had been made for me and that I have made for myself. Hoping my son would find racial belonging in Hawai'i simply because of the way we look was superficially saccharine.

On this trip, there is much eating of crunchy, syrupy shave ice by the children. Kaleidoscope flavors and colors that are so sweet, too sweet, sometimes sickly sweet. We buy at shave ice shops where it's easy to notice, standing in line, another nectarous trend: hung on the walls, pictures upon pictures of a smiling Barack Obama with shop staff. Cheerfully posed images from when the president was also a shave-ice customer during his own visits to O'ahu. Sometimes there are so many pictures they are stacked in a long column that your eye has to travel a full half-minute to take it all in. There's so much pride in these framed photos hung where everyone can see. So sweet.

Obama. The first Black US president, who has a Black birth father but grew up with his white mother in Hawai'i; whose otherness was clearly funneled through his "foreign" name too but also, obviously, through his brown skin; who endured, during his first campaign, the humiliation of religious conspiracy theories (that he was secretly Muslim) and citizenship conspiracy theories (that he was secretly a non-US citizen born in Kenya or Indonesia).

I remember the media tempest, the cyclone of head-lines. Is he Black, Mixed, both? Can you *be* both? Oh my God, what will he self-select on the census? Is he even American? Agonized, frenetic words, the probing questions of a confused public, accompanied by pictures of young Obama on the Hawaiian shores with his white grandparents, and teenage Obama playing basketball at his Hawaiian high school, the only Black boy in sight.

Obama. America's first Black president. The same president during whose two terms the US saw a meteoric, inspirational rise of the Black Lives Matter movement. Also the same president who got more death threats than any other president and whose time in office was immediately countered by white America's giant middle finger, the election of 45.

So sweet.

At first, I do—I drink the proverbial Kool-Aid. I mistake these Obama pictures as a better entry point for me and my son to develop deeper racial understanding of O'ahu rather than in the superficiality of finding people who simply look like us. I imagine, to different degrees, we are all celebrating the election of the same president with "the funny name" who grew up in this place; an election that, while not perfect, cannot help but be a milestone in the fight to dismantle racism.

And yet in Hawai'i, ultimately, there's something confounding in these shave-ice-shop pictures of our first president of color which signal, but don't resolve, complexing conflicts between "mainland" and "local," racism and post-racial utopia. *So sweet.* Stuff is clearly seamed together strangely, like a glove with the thumb affixed where the pinky should be. One can't figure how to put the damn thing on, though it's meant to be worn.

In my first book, I worked expressly to call out white supremacy, center Blackness, and show how any oppression of non-Black Asian Mixed people like me and my family is still necessarily connected to the pervasive anti-Black racism that founded and continues to uphold this empire we call the United States. As I see it, we have an enormous responsibility to acknowledge the forced suffering and sacrifices of Black people that built our country. We also owe an unpayable debt of gratitude to the stalwart resistance of African Americans and their unremitting fight to dismantle white supremacy—a collective resilience and brilliance that continues to lead the way in transformative change-making, here and worldwide, from which we all benefit. As the great civil rights leader Fannie Lou Hamer famously said, "Nobody's free till everybody's free."

You would think, given that the first Black president is from Oʻahu, where one of the largest US Asian Mixed populations resides (one that prides itself on multicultural globalism and racial tolerance), that *this* would be the ideal locale to find a model for antiracism in people who look like me and my son. Not so at all, I come to find out. It's like the exact opposite. Obama is a big deal in Hawaiʻi, and yet somehow, political understanding here has almost entirely divorced itself from conversations about anti-Blackness and systemic racism. In fact, everyday folk generally don't talk about racism at all, because in this "majority minority" multiethnic place, we outsiders are instructed by hegemony, race is not a lens through which Hawai'i can be perceived.

Meanwhile, in blatant hypocrisy, Native Hawaiian culture and language is appropriated and cheapened, and a false language of post-racial paradise is used by tourism, government, and military occupiers to promote erasure of Native Hawaiian people in a manner perfectly synchronized with anti-Black and -Brown racism and the erasure of Native Americans on the continent. It's agonizing beyond belief to see the way people here deceive themselves and that so many of those people *do* look like me.

So sweet.

Such a twisted manipulation, this cloying claim of racial harmony amidst glaring neocolonial racism. Divorcing Hawai'i from the fight for justice on the continent, preventing solidarity, engendering infighting, spreading reductive stereotypes that encourage inter-group resentment, keeping the most marginalized isolated from each other. These are "the master's tools" and, as Audre Lorde wisely predicted (and which apparently can't be restated enough) those tools are failing miserably to dismantle the master's house.

By supporting Black Lives, our ea [life, breath, land, and sovereignty] is enhanced. As a sovereign people we are saying we will stand as an example to those that would do us all harm, that their old tricks can no longer divide us. There is nothing more threatening to the state than mass solidarity across race, class and gender differences because there are far more of us . . . Onipaʻa ana ka pono—let the right stand firm.

— JOY ENOMOTO,
"Where Will You Be?: Why Black Lives Matter
in the Hawaiian Kingdom" (2017)

Kauai, island of love
Lovely princess of the islands
Kauai, island of love
Listen, can't you hear her calling
Aloha welcome my love
Her palm trees gently do the hula
While her slaves, the waves
Rush in to kiss her shores
Heaven is another name for
Kauai, island of love

— "ISLAND OF LOVE,"
Sid Tepper and Roy C. Bennet,
performed by Elvis Presley in Blue Hawai'i *(1961)*

CHAPTER NINE

Waves

Our trip is almost over. Still haven't found a damn coconut. Instead, we find sweet coconut shave ice with glorious foam on top. Days following, the tabloids trumpet a fanfare: some reality-TV couple has just passed through this same shave-ice place on their brassy, flashy babymoon. The music is so loud I'm drowning in it. I'll think about how much these white celebs, famous for nothing, got paid for an exclusive gallery of being white tourists in Hawai'i. I'll also think that shave-ice place is going to do great business. Great business...

It's thinking time on Kaua'i. I'm sitting on the balcony of our hotel room watching a pink, orange, and yellow sunrise. The roosters are crowing. The horizon is scribbled with palm silhouettes. Gorgeous. I barely need to describe it because it's everything "mainlanders" have been told about this place. Everything we see in the fantasy of our mind's eye.

We're staying on the east side in Kapa'a, a dense tourist area. Not as much fun. There's a plastic veneer covering everything so that I can't get a feel for what this place is. My white girlfriend isn't helpful. She lived here for fourteen years and can't seem to convey a grasp on this place either. "Life is so easy here," she replies when I ask if she'd ever move back. "It just cruises."

I think about how residents tell me it's so difficult to find meaningful work in Hawai'i, or work at all; about poverty and all the displaced and decimated Kānaka Maoli. Kānaka activist Loretta Ritte said, in a 2009 interview on the Mo'olelo Aloha 'Āina project website: "Everybody told me Hawaiians were stupid, Hawaiians were lazy, Hawaiians were good for not'in'. That's how I grew up, raised on Kaua'i. That's what they told us Hawaiians."

Life is so easy here? It just cruises? I don't know what my white girlfriend is talking about.

I see Brown people serving at food trucks and restaurants, dancing hula at hotels, playing ukulele at kitschy restaurants. But they're workers, entertainers, in the margins of our experience here. I don't know where they live, and this island experience we're having is a universe away from them. *Can you make a living dancing hula here?* I speculated last night watching Brown hotel hula dancers in Po'ipū, an area heavily developed for tourists despite vibrant antieviction protests. I watch the dancers more. They're smiling and putting on a show. *Are they happy doing this work? How much of their culture has been perverted by those in power to make it palatable for a white and settler tourist audience?* I don't know the answers to these things. I'm on the outside.

I remember visiting, as a child tourist, the Polynesian Cultural Center on O'ahu: wandering around half-interested, feeling like it was just another theme park; awkward in the stiffness of being a voyeur; watching, consuming people performing their own culture in a place that felt like a zoo. The women were striking and exotic to me with their sparkling eyes, long hair, and brown skin. Which is hilarious now, as I think about it, because I probably looked more like them than like my own parents.

I'll find out this trip that the Polynesian Cultural Center (PCC) is Mormon. Which will totally baffle me. "Owned by The Church of Jesus Christ of Latter-day Saints (LDS Church)," writes a white male faculty member of Brigham Young University-Hawai'i, upon whose campus the Center is built. "The LDS Church teaches self-sufficiency." It was opened, I read more online, to provide employment and scholarships for students at Brigham Young University Hawai'i and to preserve the cultures of Polynesia. "The college students needed money, as did the townfolk, and the answer was to create a tourist attraction and to work very, very hard." That seems like a good thing, I reflect. "If you haven't been to the PCC—make it a part of your next trip to Hawaii."

But then I keep reading other sources online. I read about the first ten Mormon missionaries who came to Hawai'i in 1850, three years before a missionary-introduced smallpox epidemic would almost entirely wipe out the Native population. "The Utah elders interfered with efforts of authorities to deal with the disease, claiming it was part of the 'scourges' accompanying the imminent Second Coming, and promising that their healing powers (priesthood 'administrations') would protect the native saints." These early missionaries were all men, I assume all white men. I think about that Center again; about missionaries, colonization, conversion, Indigeneity, white supremacy. And I'm not so sure what "good" means.

In our Kaua'i hotel, tourists are waking up now. Doors opening and closing with quiet clicks. Footsteps on the stairs, in the hallways, on the pavement. Cars backing out of parking spaces, rolling slowly toward the main road. All traces of orange and pink have faded from the sky. A few confused roosters are still crowing. It's only 6:13 a.m. There will be many more bodies soon. I feel suddenly tired. The same tired I felt in Seattle anticipating the day, the city, the traffic, the whiteness.

Years ago, when my husband and I were shameless, oblivious Kaua'i tourists, we drank sweet mai tais on the beach every day at noon. More or less. Why do they taste so good in Hawai'i? *They don't taste like this in Seattle,* we would announce giddily to ourselves. This time we want to have those mai tais again. "Somehow it feels wrong that I haven't had a mai tai yet," my husband says. It's a goal of his and, if I'm honest, a goal of mine too. A happy memory we want to relive that's clearly about more than just rum and juice.

Thanks to my friend, who offers to watch our son, we get the gift of a rare dinner date. It's my fault. I suggest it. Seems like a silly, fun idea. Something we should do, like the myriad of obligatory SoCal theme parks I visited growing up. We go to a tacky tourist restaurant named after Paradise. There's music, singing, an ukulele being played upon a small stage again. Their low-shelf mai tai is $12.50. The high-shelf one is $14.50. The price tag feels shocking, but we order anyway. The drinks might be good, but really they just don't taste the same as when we were younger. The drinks together with a not-great dinner cost overall more than a hundred dollars. We don't say it out loud, but we both feel a little depressed.

On a different night, for a different dinner, we do something entirely the opposite. We hit up a popular-with-"locals" burrito joint. Hole in the wall. There's a line—handful of tourists, but a lot of brown, browner, and dark-brown residents. It's called Da Crack, which I don't get at first. Then I see the sign over the takeout window. A chubby Mexican man wearing a white tank top, sombrero atop his head, sits cross-legged, playing guitar to the sunset. A scorpion scutters through the red dirt behind him, drawing attention to the fact that, oblivious or uncaring, he is wearing his pants so low he has plumber's butt. There's no indication the man is drinking, but I imagine he's drunk—the sign so perfectly plays into the stereotype.

I'm guessing "Da Crack" is also reference to how people say, when something's really good, it's addictive "like crack."

Burritos, drugs, Mexico, Mexicans. They tell me this is Hawai'i-style humor, working-class and ethnic humor, charming in its own way. But I'm thinking about having grown up in California, which has the largest Latinx population in the nation. I remember hearing Spanish around me all the time. I remember the Mexican food trucks, the Latina nannies and housecleaners (often undocumented) the many Latino men, day laborers (also undocumented), working at construction projects in upscale neighborhoods.

I remember crossing the border in San Diego to visit Tijuana and the energetic attempts by locals there to capture tourist money with kitschy gifts, street food, cheap pharmaceuticals, and other things. I remember seeing shacks, poverty, what seemed like extremely unsafe and unsanitary living conditions. I remember hearing about the corruption of Mexico and how you never wanted to get caught by the Mexican police. I remember crossing the border back into the United States. Walls, fear, barbed wire, scowling border patrol, cowering pedestrians.

I remember the Latinx family at my son's public school in Seattle that was brave enough to come forward, in a room filled with privileged, mostly white folks, and talk about how scared they were of being deported, post–45 election. They cried and their voices shook.

Given these memories, I find myself unable to accept this Kaua'i burrito stand's anti-Latinx humor as "charming" simply because it's authored by so-called "locals" in a place where barely any Latinos live. I don't find it charming and don't know if I ever could.

Not too long after this trip, 45 and his administration will officially end DACA, a program that protected nearly 800,000 young undocumented immigrants brought to the US as children. The program will not accept any more applications. Those whose permits expire before March 5, 2018 will be eligible to reapply for an extra two years of protected status. But hundreds of thousands of people whose permits expire after March 5 will be eligible for deportation as early as the next day. Congress will have only six months to do something, but no one will feel optimistic.

By April 2018, under a "zero-tolerance policy," 45 and his administration will begin aggressively prosecuting as many southern-border-crossing offenses as possible, a move that quickly becomes an egregious abuse of human rights and a deplorable humanitarian crisis.

Over the next two months, as Latinx parents, fleeing homeland strife, are detained en masse attempting to enter the US, more than 2,300 of their migrant children are forcibly separated from them. Parents are sent to detention facilities while children are caged, moved into overflow tent facilities, then flown around the country into the care of relatives, shelters, organizations, and foster homes. After nationwide uproar, 45 signs a policy rescinding his policy, but there is no plan to reunite the devastated Latinx parents with their little ones.

The sun is coming up bright and hot. I'm about to move back into our air-conditioned hotel room, I suppose. It's just I feel so cut off in there. Sprinklers come on. *There are sprinklers here?* The sound of the water spitting in checkered pattern back and forth across the hotel's manicured gardens reminds me of waking up every day, growing up, to sprinklers in SoCal's wealthier neighborhoods. But SoCal is desert, dry and dusty, so watering makes sense, in a wasteful way. It seems funny to have sprinklers on Kaua'i, which boasts the second wettest spot on Earth.

I go inside our room.

At Heiva I Kaua'i International Tahitian Dance Competition in Kapa'a Beach Park, I smile when they announce where the dancers are from. One group is from California, like me. The dance is incredibly beautiful, and some of the dancers are as young as my son. I note that to him. He doesn't respond, but he also doesn't want to stop watching. I think about *Moana*, that sweeping animated movie musical about the Pacific Islands, that just came out and enraptured America's children. Then I remember it's a Disney movie helmed by white people and feel distressed. *Fucking that was my first thought? God, Sharon. So colonized.*

I think there are more white people on Kaua'i than on O'ahu. My friend runs into someone she knows, a white Rastafarian. He has dreads, a big belly, his clothes are ratty. He carries an old umbrella that he uses only some of the time. He's too tan. "My friend's in a reggae band," she tells us. *Of course he is.* I haven't met a white rasta hippy like this for a long time. Not since I lived in Cali. There are tons of them there in Venice Beach, Malibu, at desert raves and Burning Man—smelling of patchouli oil, high on weed, mushrooms, acid, and ecstasy, deeply suspicious of the fluoride in tap water, which is surely a conspiracy to control our minds.

White Rasta in this moment is with his sun-bleached blond five-year-old. Doesn't pay much attention to the boy, though. He takes a conference call with his other kids by a different mother, while my friend watches his here-and-now son. I can't tell if this babysitting arrangement was something they agreed on in advance or if it's something he just decided she was going to do for him. Either way. It's happening.

The bright-blond boy tries to play with our Mixed boys, but it doesn't click much. He leaves to play on his own, tries to drag a huge piece of driftwood into a surf that could smash his small frame. My friend stops him and explains why it isn't safe. White Rasta is still on his conference call with his other kids, sitting in the sand, propped against the trunk of a palm tree. Blond Boy ends up wandering away down the shore. He turns into an even tinier body capped with bright hair, looking down, shuffling in the sand. *What is he thinking about?*

He never looks back. My friend watches carefully, eventually has to go after him because he goes too far. I see her bringing him slowly back, talking to him. I reflect on what she might be saying.

At dinner we end up at the same restaurant, Mermaids. "Fancy seeing you guys here," White Rasta says, friendly. My insides curdle. An Asian woman takes our order. My friend tells us this place has good eats. But it's white-people food cooked by a Brown man. I get a coconut curry to which I end up adding so much soy sauce I might have just drunk straight out of the bottle. *I make better coconut curry than this at home.* "I know," my husband replies in a low voice. We don't say anything too loud because we don't want to be rude. My friend has been kind to us here. So we eat quietly while White Rasta talks with my friend about his chickens (he has fourteen baby chicks currently) and how he became vegan.

My husband elbows me discreetly and motions to look behind my back. There's a mural of a white woman mermaid with light eyes, a tiny waist, and seashells cupping her oversized breasts. Barbie mermaid. We're sitting in a cramped space and the mural is so close she looks huge, larger than life, distorted. I'm disgusted and want to get out of here. To his credit, White Rasta does try to check in with us a couple times. He's trying to be welcoming in his laid-back white island way. But I don't believe him. I can't help thinking about those old white men in the public-pool hot tub back home. I either smile with pressed lips, nod my head tersely, or give short answers.

Saying goodbye, he tells us he's going to be on the radio tonight. We never tune in.

Again it feels like there are more white people living on Kaua'i than on O'ahu. But maybe, I surmise, it's because we're in the company of a white friend on this leg of the trip, whereas we spent all our time on O'ahu with Asian friends. One sure way to find out: I look it up. Kaua'i County: 33.3 percent white; Honolulu County: 22.2 percent white. Definitely not my imagination. Definitely more white folks on Kaua'i. I contemplate how that came to be, exactly.

My white friend says she likes this beach, it's a good one. So I look forward to it with my forward-moving steps. But when we get there, the sand of the beach has a nasty rash. Irritated, itchy, painful. Underneath and over the grains and layers of its sandy skin are bumps, hives, sometimes open sores, gashes. Looking up and down the shoreline, I can't feel relaxed here. This place is so visibly unhappy, afflicted by the pieces of people's lives that got thrown into the sea and washed ashore with the waves to make a misery here.

"There's so much trash," I finally remark out loud.

"Yeah"—my white friend nods—"it's garbage washed in mostly from Japan."

That turns out not to be true. Most of the litter, explains an expert with the Hawai'i Department of Land and Natural Resources in a press interview, is everyday items tossed on the ground or into the water from "just about anywhere and everywhere." But at the time I don't know that. Instead, I look up at my Nisei Mixed husband and Sansei Mixed son, who have run to play with the ocean. I don't know what else to do but pull out my camera. I crouch and creep across the sad sand, not to take pictures of the foamy water sweeping across it, but to commemorate all the shit that has come to pollute it, allegedly from my husband and son's ancestral land.

Like my son, I'm a swimmer and in love with water. First, as a young child, it was baths so long my fingers pruned and the temperature dropped to cold. Then, the lake in Massachusetts we visited every summer with my white cousins; canoeing, raft jumping, catching frogs, splashing and diving from morning till night. When we flew overseas to visit family in Taiwan, I couldn't wait for eggy-smelling sulfur baths in the mountains, a smell my sister abhorred but that beckoned to me. When we moved to China for a year, though, there wasn't much access to water. I do recollect being enamored with an indoor hotel pool somewhere. Then we moved to Southern California, and it was the ocean: stroking with the waves, always swimming out a little too far, going in and under even when the water was frigid.

When it was time to leave California, as an adult, I found myself in Seattle, where Lake Washington, Lake Union, and the Puget Sound envelop the urban landscape in a wide embrace. I can almost always see water anywhere I am, and can lake-swim in the summer again, this time with my boy. And now too, battling muscle armoring and chronic pain from the hard times, I'm back to baths and the pool, like when I was younger.

This is all to say that water has always been where I find my personal peace and my healing. It's what I always go back to, wherever I am. Sometimes this intense draw feels mysterious to me. But then it's worth remembering, I nudge myself occasionally, that my Taiwanese family goes back many generations on Taiwan, an island nation surrounded by the sea. Maybe not so mysterious after all. Either way, on this Hawai'i trip, as in trips past, the ocean will be one of the only places where I can feel the most natural connection.

I've encountered honu (sea turtles) underwater three times in my life—always alone, though others were nearby, and only while snorkeling in Hawai'i. Honu are one of the oldest kinds of creatures on earth and excellent navigators, said to have guided the first Polynesians to the Hawaiian islands. This time, on Kaua'i, it's our second-to-last day. My son is coming down with something and doesn't feel like swimming much, and my husband doesn't really like snorkeling.

So I take off on my own for a half hour. I try to swim near rocks and coral, where there are more fish. At one point, however, I find myself drifting across a long, empty stretch where there's nothing but sand, and I get bored. I stroke a couple more times, about to veer sharply away from this ocean prairie, when something suddenly rises before me in a dust of water and sand. *What the hell.* I stop and tread water, the sand clears, and there he is. Calm, relaxed, unaffected, going about his business, living as his ancestors have lived for eons before him. I watch, enthralled, for as long as I can stand it before popping to the surface and frantically looking for someone to share with. I see a white woman swimming by.

"Hey!" I say excitedly, motioning. "There's a sea turtle here if you want to see him, I can show you!"

The white woman smiles, uninterested. "Oh, that's okay," she says, polite but indifferent. "I live here and I've seen him a million times." She moves on. My face falls some. Then I shrug, dive back down, watch honu a bit more before rushing back to my husband and son to tell all. It is a privilege to be near and in the water every day, one that's enormously complicated by the fact of me being a tourist on stolen land. Being close to the ocean makes me happy; it's the thing I love the most now, and the thing I'll miss the most when I go home. I'm just not sure how to reconcile that love with the reality of my not-belonging.

Our last beach visit is the best beach visit. It's a bumpy ride, then a small hike in. Not far, but far enough to deter many tourists. We park in an empty dirt lot and walk along a dry, dusty road where the sun beats down and mosquitoes nip at our skin. We hear the dull roar of the ocean but can't see anything until at last the brush parts and there she is: kai, vast and moving and rolling before us. The beach is practically deserted, quiet, sloping down to the sea and, to the right, around a corner. The blue sky, lewa, is colossal and endless above.

At the trailhead, someone has hung pieces of white coral from a tree with blue string. It's carefully done, so careful that it could almost be art. *Click. Click.* My camera. I try to frame the ocean in the background of the shot, but for some reason can't get the right angle. Never mind. *Tied to this string. Click. Click.*

We settle in at this place for some time. Swimming and snorkeling, resting, then swimming and snorkeling again. I'm grateful for the peace and quiet finally. It feels hard to find this kind of peace and quiet in Hawaiʻi, even as the islands are, ironically, marketed to us visitors as the tranquil tropics we've always been looking for. Capitalism, tourism, and militarism have spread notably more than when I was child visitor here, only a couple decades ago.

"I think this might be the beach where we got married," my husband reflects. But we're not sure. We decide to hike around the corner to see if that helps. We gather our things and walk lazily, slowly, through the sand, pausing frequently, sometimes moving into the water to look at rocks and sea creatures. My son finds various treasures: burnt wood, lava rock, tiny bits of coral, sticks and special stones. It's inspiring, watching him embrace the natural world like an old friend, in that special way children can, still untouched by the weight of adulthood.

After rounding the corner, we see even more beach snaking and unwinding for a distance ahead. Still mostly deserted. But my son and his friend are too tired to go any farther. My husband and I shrug. That's how things go when you have kids. We settle in again. Rest under the shade, play in the happy sand, dance with the incoming surf.

In my beach selfies here, I look like a different person. Younger. Calm. Rested. Peaceful. I feel sad, because when I take selfies at home I look wretched, distressed, older than my age. My face written in premature lines. My skin uneven, spotted, pale. At home I feel trapped by stress and anxiety in our greedy, exploding city. Amazon, Microsoft, Google, Facebook. Some people call it "Silicon Seattle." I can never manage to get in the car and get out of the city. I get stuck.

Yet it's funny how faraway is never as far as it seems. This time when we're on Kaua'i, driving to go snorkeling, the homes suddenly turn jaw-dropping, outrageous, gorgeous. So rich. "This is where Facebook Guy is being a dick and pushing people off their land," my husband says.

"Who, Mark Zuckerberg?" I ask.

"Yeah," he answers.

I'm quiet, thinking about that and about so-called Silicon Seattle. I'm also thinking about the fact that Zuckerberg has an Asian American wife. And two Mixed Race daughters.

My husband and I make one last effort to figure it all out. Where was that place we got married? We stand puzzling, contemplating the shoreline, while small waves lap at our toes. Finally, we think we see it. Way far ahead. The spot. So far away it appears in soft focus, like a dreamy watercolor painting. We wanted to reprise the wedding picture of us holding hands, walking in the surf, now with our son in between us. But there's no way the boys have energy to walk that far, so we abort mission, shrugging again. We take a happy selfie instead, pack up, and head back to the car.

This time he drives. And for the moment,

I try to quiet
this Mixed mind
churning with so many questions.

As Tūtū Pele flows through man-made cities, she does not ask permission to take what is rightfully hers. She commands you to recognize her mighty strength and bow down to her power. She does not pass by and apologize; she does what is naturally her right. Instead, you must apologize to her and thank her for borrowing her 'āina (land) for that fabulous period of time you were able to live there. Slowly, yet purposefully, she sets all on fire that happen to be in her way, including your home and belongings . . . Pele is not inviting. Pele's home is dangerous, sacred, and forbidding. We know not when she will present herself next and demonstrate her mighty power.

— MANU KA'IAMA,
"Kū i ka Pono: The Movement Continues,"
A Nation Rising: Hawaiian Movements
for Life, Land, and Sovereignty *(2014)*

Most people live on a lonely island,
Lost in the middle of a foggy sea.
Most people long for another island,
One where they know they will like to be.

Bali Ha'i may call you,
Any night, any day,
In your heart, you'll hear it call you:
"Come away ... Come away."

Bali Ha'i will whisper
On the wind of the sea:
"Here am I, your special island!
Come to me, come to me!"

— "BALI HA'I,"
Richard Rodgers and Oscar Hammerstein II,
South Pacific *(1958)*

CHAPTER TEN

Circle to Center

Finally we find one. I buy it street-side for seven dollars, which seems expensive. But I sang my son this fairytale lullaby. A Brown woman hacks the fruit open expertly, sticks in a straw, doesn't smile. She was busy and seems annoyed at the interruption. Her hands pass the hairy brown orb to me, and I hand it to my son. At last. His face lights up. He carries and drinks from it lovingly. Yet there isn't much juice inside, compared with how large the fruit is. It's gone quickly. He wants more, but we aren't getting another one. And I suddenly realize my lullaby, in the end, has shifted key…

On May 3, 2018, as I'm in the final stages of editing this book, Mount Kilauea erupts. It erupts continuously for weeks, spewing 250 million cubic meters of lava, destroying more than 700 homes and forcing over 2,000 people to evacuate. It is one of the largest eruptions in Hawaiʻi in decades. The Halemaumau Crater of Kilauea, where Hawaiian fire goddess Pelehonuamea makes her home, doubles in size. Kānaka Maoli leave hoʻokupu (offerings) such as food, drink, hula, leaves, and lei, expressing reverence and gratitude for their fiery deity. Some believe Tūtū Pele is growing angry with outsiders settling on the Big Island. "She's going to do what she's doing, she's cleaning house," a Hawaiian resident tells *Hawaii News Now*. "She's just making right. She's doing what she needs to do for the community."

Right before we left Oʻahu, the boys were romping with the sea, joyous, ecstatic, euphoric. When on land they played too, but also eventually bickered over various typical things: iPad time, boredom, turn-taking. The ocean, however—she brought them seemingly unlimited harmony, even as they moved their bodies endlessly. They never bickered with each other, or with her, while they swam.

Uncle and I watched contentedly because, simple truth, parents love to see their children happy. It fills our hearts like nothing else can, or ever will, in life. I remarked warmly how much the boys loved the sea. Uncle nodded with smiling eyes, agreed. "And every time they're in the water," he adds, "they're connecting more and more with Pele."

Pele.

Suddenly I'm flooded with bizarre memories.

Pele.

When I was in middle and high school in the nineties, I was obsessed with the music of Tori Amos. She sang and played piano, like I did, was classically trained, like me, but she managed to make music in ways that broke beyond whiteness, which I had never been allowed to do. She was the only prominent example I could see of a woman using the instruments we shared to tell her unapologetic truth in sweet, sharp edges and bright broken glass. She was unlike anyone else out there at the time.

Tori reads as a white woman; her father is a white Methodist pastor, but she is also of Indigenous descent, born to a Native American Mixed mother whose lineage brings together two Eastern Cherokee lines. While Tori's paternal white Christian family had staunch, strict expectations of the behavior and role she would assume as a woman, her maternal Native family taught her stories of her ancestors, with values like strength, courage, respect for the land, and the importance of finding her own voice.

She wrote and sang about all these conflicts in her music, which could be as angelic and ethereal as it was fierce, turbulent, and jagged. She challenged the colonialism, patriarchy, misogyny, and racism of white America and white American Christendom. And I loved her for it.

But in 1996, Tori Amos released her third studio album, *Boys for Pele*.

It was the year I graduated from my shitty, almost-all-white high school—the high school that was too small, that I hated, where I had no friends, where I felt alone and couldn't wait to leave. And it was the first time I felt confused, uncomfortable, and rather cheerless about my music idol.

Pele.

A goddess I didn't know at first—but when I learned, glancing back at Tori's album, something curled up tightly inside me. Even then, though I knew I would never belong to the islands, I understood that I was still connected to Hawai'i because of the body I live in and that, through the connection, I had some sort of accountability and complicated relationship to the place, its people, and for myself, all at once.

Tori Amos had discovered Pele during a one-week trip to O'ahu while visiting a friend she described as "a medicine woman, a very wise woman." At the time, Tori was reevaluating her relationship with masculinity after a long stretch in the music business working alongside men. Walking up and down the beaches of the North Shore with this medicine woman, she explained in an *Everybody's News* interview, "I just began to feel the presence of Pele all over the island, even though I know she's not on that island." Tori felt a flame alight within herself. She conceived of a new album about stealing fire from the men in her life as well as a journey to finding her own fire as a woman.

Yet the cover of *Boys for Pele* is a palette of grays and faded blues, except for the songstress's fiery red hair. It is dusty, dirty, dry. The ocean is nowhere. Tori Amos sits on the deck of a tin-roofed shack in an old wooden rocking chair, cradling a rifle in her hands. Some kind of game she has presumably hunted hangs lifeless from the rafter behind her. On the back of the album, sitting on the same deck in the same chair, she holds a small piglet like a human infant (a piglet she is also pictured breastfeeding in another image).

There appears to be nothing in this imagery that signals Hawai'i or Hawaiian land, or pays respect to the Hawaiian people and their mythology, which Tori Amos borrowed from so freely to fuel her own feminist fire and sell her album. *But as an Indigenous Mixed woman, isn't that her right?* I ponder. As a non-Indigenous woman, I can't answer that question. But as a non-Hawaiian Mixed woman who has similarly sought sense-of-self as a tourist in Hawai'i, I feel ill at ease.

Besides Tori, in middle and high school, there was grunge: Nirvana, Pearl Jam, Soundgarden, Stone Temple Pilots. In college, there were pop princesses: Britney Spears, Christina Aguilera, Jessica Simpson, Mandy Moore. There were catchy boy bands like Boyz II Men and NSYNC. Michael Jackson was still going, Aaliyah was still alive, Beyoncé was just getting started, and Missy Elliott was at the top of her game.

There were a lot of white performers, naturally. There were Black performers and some Latinx. There were no Asians or Mixed Asian people like me making top-forty anything on the radio. At least, not as far as I could tell, and certainly in no prominent way. This pop-culture invisibility didn't escape my notice. It's just that when you have no power or control, you learn to resign yourself and push your disappointment down to a dark recess, where it will hopefully be forgotten and never really is.

But then, at the turn of the millennium, there was a shift. Which also did not escape my notice. Michelle Branch (Indonesian/white American) released the hit "Everywhere." KT Tunstall (Chinese/white Scot) broke through with "Black Horse and the Cherry Tree." Actor and singer Vanessa Hudgens (Filipina/Native American/white) became the star of *High School Musical*. And Nicole Scherzinger (Native Hawaiian/Filipino/white) became the frontwoman of the girl group Pussycat Dolls.

There was something extra special for me about Scherzinger's stardom. One, that a visibly Mixed

Hawaiian Asian woman could be seen as successful leading a troupe of five other women (four of whom were white) was mind-blowing. Two, the group was built on a burlesque girl-power concept that was irresistible, and the way Nicole seemed to embrace her Brown Mixed body, her power and sexuality within this concept, was captivating. She looked so cool, so confident, so inspiring. She was standing out as her Mixed self and owning her truth.

So I devoured the Pussycat Dolls' music videos and live performances online. I danced and sang along and rejoiced. I turned up their music every time it came on the radio. *There's my girl! What's up, Mixed sister!* Pride. Elation. Triumph.

Representation matters. Or so they say.

But turns out it really does need to be the right kind of representation.

Didn't take long before I started noticing … other things.

In the tabloids, there were always pictures of Nicole Scherzinger in bikinis, in Hawai'i. Granted, the tabloids routinely follow celebrities on their vacations to tropical places. But there seemed to be an inordinate number of photos of Scherzinger, wet in the ocean, somewhere on the islands. I guessed it was because she was Brown and Hawaiian. Anyway, there was no mistaking that the media really liked to see her as an "island girl," although she mostly grew up in Louisville, Kentucky. And leveraging her Hawaiian Mixed racial otherness—without paying authentic respect to her Kānaka roots—apparently was the best way to do that.

Case in point: after a while, Nicole Scherzinger announced she would be releasing a debut solo album titled *Her Name Is Nicole.* "Whatever U Like" was one of four album singles released in advance. In the video for the song, Scherzinger is assaulted at night by a group of masked men who kidnap her and put her in a box. Post-abduction, she variously appears dancing hula, writhing on hot stones, covered naked in clay, doing yoga in a minidress, or swimming in a white bathing suit, all the while singing lyrics like:

> I'll do whatever you like
> I'll do whatever you like
> I can do, I can do, I do, I do whatever you
> like

It was not a very popular song. In fact, all four released singles from what was supposed to be this first solo album did not do well, and in the end the entire project was shelved at Scherzinger's request. She shifted back to the Pussycat Dolls ,and the group came out with "Right There." In the video for the song, Nicole, scantily dressed, dances hula again, this time while singing:

> Me like the way that he put it on me
> Me like the way that he push up on me
> Me like the way that he goin' down

I didn't see much improvement, or any at all.

The following year, Scherzinger made her Hollywood acting debut. She played a bit role in *Men in Black 3* as Boris the Animal's girlfriend. Appearing briefly at the beginning of the film, Scherzinger's character, wearing thigh-high stiletto boots and a low-cut black dress, carries a jiggling cake, backgrounded by her ample cleavage, into a space-station prison to visit her boyfriend. Upon being escorted to Boris's cell, the two characters make out grossly and Scherzinger helps Boris break free. But she is quickly betrayed when Boris blasts a hole in the station and allows Scherzinger to get sucked into space, quipping, "Sorry, darling. We did love the cake." Her character never has a name, and Scherzinger is credited at the end of the film only as "Boris's Girlfriend."

I remember the heartbreak so well, the feeling of cold humiliation and crushing defeat that washed over me as I watched this woman I wanted to admire get reduced by the industry to a sexed cut of meat. I could suddenly see that the trajectory set for Scherzinger by the Pussycat Dolls was not as positive as I had imagined it to be. I also remember not feeling that surprised, because these sorts of highly gendered, fetishized outcomes are what *I* had been taught to expect for myself, as a Mixed Woman, my whole life.

Over time, Nicole Scherzinger has claimed a more truthful space for herself, liberated from neatly packaged deceit. She has begun to publicly acknowledge battling deep body insecurity as a teenager and bulimia throughout her twenties, including, in large part, during her time with the Pussycat Dolls. In interviews, Scherzinger describes the experience of her eating disorder as a "horribly paralyzing disease" and an imprisoning "dark time" that "stole all of my happiness, confidence, and memories." She hadn't wanted to come out to fans originally, admitted Nicole, because she was ashamed.

Notwithstanding, Nicole Scherzinger is still a celebrity; one who seems to have redefined her professional path through sheer hard work and perseverance. She continues to sing on occasion, voices the mother in Moana, and has also leveraged her natural ability to move into a dance career. When I see these changes, I feel some peace. And also, I admire this Mixed woman again, but now for her grace, determination, and persistence, despite it all.

At various times throughout my life, I too have indulged in fantasies and reveries about Hawai'i. I have fantasized about tropical visits—the ones I've taken and the ones I want to take. The ocean, the beaches, the mountains are breathtaking, and I have imagined myself somehow magically connected to the land. I have fantasized about living in Hawai'i, assuming it would be easy and comfortable. The pan-Asian settler culture fits my family like a glove, I reason. "Locals" assume we live there. We blend in.

But only superficially, I realize now.

What a fantastic, plastic reverie.

It has taken a while to circle to center; to rifle through the complex, interwoven mess of tales I have been taught about myself and Hawai'i; to find the inmost kernel at the interior, a true starting point to clarify myself and my racialized body while visiting in this place.

I may not know the islands barely at all, but being on Indigenous land while its people have been erased is entirely familiar. It's not something that goes away anywhere, let's be honest. In Seattle, upon traditional territories of the Duwamish, certainly not. In Toronto recently, upon lands of the Mississauga, also the same. When I launched my first book tour in Vancouver, BC, ancestral home of the Musqueam, Squamish and Tsleil-Waututh, same again. Even as a child in Taiwan, island of the Taiwanese aborigines, still the same.

In reality, Hawai'i is painfully militarized, overrun by tourism, and suffocated by the willful ignorance of settlers. Light-skinned Asian Mixed people, like me, occupy an uppermost rung of the settler hierarchy and are often accessories or key culprits in a takeover that still digs a heavy heel into the neck of the land's Indigenous people. Meanwhile, there's an avoidant "Everybody's mixed" settler narrative that resists acknowledging its own racism and refuses to see that the ongoing occupation of Hawai'i is part of the same white-supremacist continuum brutalizing Black, Brown, and Native bodies on the continent.

Wouldn't moving to Hawai'i, in the oversimplified way I have always imagined, just be fulfilling my own denial, anti-Indigeneity, and even anti-Blackness? Sinking into the comfort of pretending, avoiding my own self-hatred by recklessly taking advantage of whatever privileges I can get in this mixed-racialized body; escaping a settled place only to slide on new slippers of settlerism while belligerently insisting that white supremacy isn't real because Asians and Mixed people are a majority, whites are a minority, and that anti-Blackness is a "mainland" problem.

But then again, there aren't many Black people in Seattle either. And here I am.

First thing I notice, stepping off the plane back in Seattle, is how white it is. When I was in Hawai'i I didn't think the difference was that big. But now I'm back—it's big. And I brood over how I ended up in this white place for so long.

It is a specific whiteness, though. A whiteness that pats itself on the back for being "the good white people" living the right kind of life, unpretentious, tolerant, and nature-loving, in an exceedingly "liberal" place. A granola, woodsy, hippy, Whole Foods whiteness that wears Bogs in the winter, Chacos in the summer, and jeans all year round. A whiteness that only eats organic, vegetarian, unprocessed, non-GMO, vegan, gluten- and hormone- and dairy-free; that feeds its pet dogs expensive raw diets; that shops weekly at expensive farmers' markets whose vendors comprise a surprising number of white bodies (when we know brown bodies are working those fields), but shuns local produce stands run or staffed by People of Color because the produce isn't fresh or organic enough.

Yesterday there was a violent white-supremacist riot in Charlottesville, Virginia, and a white woman died. Today the neo-Nazis hold another rally, here, downtown in Seattle. Entirely unrepentant and unremorseful. Seattle counterprotesters do turn out in the hundreds, but the Seattle police form a blockade, pepper-spraying and arresting anyone who tries to push through. I don't think the two groups ever came face-to-face. I've no doubt police intention was to prevent a repeat of Charlottesville. In some ways, I suppose, they did. But the impact, really, was that they just became bodyguards for the neo-KKK.

My editor at the South Seattle Emerald, an African American man, texts me, *"You going to the Charlottesville demonstration?"*

"Don't think so," I write back. *"Sounds dangerous."*

"Yeah it does," he agrees. *"I'm going to go to the International Festival. I think seeing so many of our people of color and immigrant communities is a mighty tribute."*

I think about that and it registers. I decide to go too, bring my son—who complains, as usual, most of the time. But I insist we stay for at least a little.

We see our neighbors, an interracial family. White mother. Alaska Native father. We see old Fijian friends. There are Black and Brown and Muslim people everywhere. The park is colorful with hijab, food, children, and smiles. I can't imagine any of this in Hawai'i. But anyway, it's been days, and the islands seem a universe away.

On the main stage they're finally ready for performances. First, youth dance from Somalia. The dancers are joyful and dynamic. The young African women vibrant and glowing. My son is still complaining. I lose my temper. Lean down. Whisper fiercely in his ear, "I would like to point out to you that a lot of these people are Muslim. The very same people who 45 doesn't like in this country. We are here to support. Show some respect." His eyes get a little wider; he nods knowingly, apologizes, grows quiet. He still doesn't want to be here. But he understands.

Next up, youth from the Pacific Islands. The dancers aren't Hawaiian, I learn, they are Fijian and Tongan.

"Look!" I exclaim to my son, trying to improve his mood. "It's like dance from Hawai'i!" There's maybe a small glimmer in his eye, but he's still sulking.

Then we hear "Hey!" from behind us and, happily, it's his Fijian friend from preschool. My son beams. The two boys sit together contentedly, but after a while they start to lose interest and head to the playground. I find the friend's Fijian mother. Big hug. We talk about our summers. "You went to Hawai'i, right?" she asks. "If you're going to go to Hawai'i, then you've got to go to Fiji." I think about that.

The Pacific Islander dancers are wrapping up. Their last dance is to a song from *Moana*. "It's about how our people traveled across the seas," explains the MC. My son magically reappears, and now he's straining to watch. He knows this movie. He loves this movie. I do too, even though it's a big studio production.

"What can you expect from a Disney movie?" said Uncle when I asked him what he thought, on O'ahu. Still, I think my Seattle son is connecting the dots, and maybe that's not so bad.

He won't admit it to me, but I think my son likes this last dance. Later we talk about how the dancers weren't Hawaiian, how there are many islands in the Pacific, and that *Moana* is a mashup, like how *Ninjago* (the only show we never let him watch) is a mashup of Chinese and Japanese. "You're a mashup too," he retorts, because he knows I'm being critical. Point taken.

And after this park visit we have one of the most profound conversations about being Mixed Race people yet. Mother to son. Son to mother. Over time, my son has had a lot of questions about what it means for us to be "part white." I keep writing, I keep reading, but still I don't really have answers for him. We just talk about it until we get tired and talk about something else. We do the best we can. I don't remember how it comes up, but it comes up again.

I say something about how being "part white" doesn't mean you're an "all white" person; that a lot of it rests on how we look, whether others see us as white or Asian; also that how we feel on the inside matters too. For example, though I have a white parent, I don't feel like an "all white" person. The same is true for my son's father.

My son speculates that all three of us—me, him, and his dad—look Asian. I agree that I think others see the Asian in us much of the time. He says he doesn't feel like an "all white" person either. *Relief.* We talk about our shared experience, the three of us, as Asian Mixed people who look like each other. I think of my white mother. I think of my husband's white father. And I'm blown away watching the reality of my son, who has no white parent (something I've been abstractly fascinated by for a long time), playing out in real time. I think about Hawai'i again.

Then he surprises me. "But Mom, I see kids who have a white parent and a Black parent, and that's confusing. Are they white or part white?" Which allows us to have a conversation about how Black Mixed children, if they look Black at all, are treated as Black people. I note that it's very different for us as light-skinned Asian Mixed people. Though there are white-passing Black children, I add, and that can be hard if those children don't feel white on the inside. He gets it. I know this conversation happened because we were just in a space filled with Black and Brown people. It dawns on me that if we were from the islands, where the deceitful "Everyone's Mixed so nobody's anything" mythology has come to dominate, we might never have had this conversation.

I question my need to decide which is the "better" place from which to dismantle and unpack racism, when so many places have been touched by white colonialism. There is no such place. There is also a way I'm still learning to sing a song to myself; one of forgiveness and compassion, resilience and hope. Our bodies do not always end up where we would like to be, where we imagine we belong, or where we do belong. Sometimes we don't have a choice. You fight where you are, wherever you find yourself.

Home

It's seven a.m. in Seattle on a seventy-degree morning. Days have passed. Hawai'i drifts in my mind, further and further away. A dream. Another hazy memory. When I asked my Native Hawaiian friend what she didn't miss about Seattle, she said, "I don't miss the whiteness." She added, "And the traffic." Two days back, I feel the whiteness pressing in around me like a bottleneck. There are so many white people here. They're everywhere.

The brown of my skin is fading away. I know it's wrong?—but I'm sad to see it go. I walk my mutt to the dog park and don't wear sunscreen, just to hold on a little more. *Remember how high those melanoma rates are in Washington? It's precisely because of what you are doing in this moment.* Well. Not exactly. Melanoma's high in Washington because there are a lot of white people who don't think they need sunscreen when the weather's mostly cloudy, not because a Biracial girl got brown in a place where people conclude her body belongs and she's trying to cling to that belonging.

I look at my fading brown skin and feel despondent. *Tans go away.* But if I lived on the islands, this skin wouldn't leave me. That would be my skin. And people wouldn't see me as "having a tan," they would see me as … what I am?

This afternoon I'm having lunch with a good friend. It's hard to make time to see people. For various reasons. Some of them good reasons, some of them not. We're texting, trying to figure out where to eat in the neighborhood. There are a lot of choices. We toss around Thai food, Vietnamese food. Then she writes, "Poke?" She's never been to this new place nearby and, she adds, "I'd rather try it with someone who likes poke."

Do you like poke? Although this time it's not a "local" asking, it's a "mainlander." I mull over why my friend automatically assumed I eat poke and that going to this restaurant with me would be a more comfortable introduction for her. No. I don't mull at all. I know why.

My face is starting to look old again, the lines on my forehead and between my brows more etched. I took a non-beach selfie yesterday. I looked so tired. Again. I miss Hawai'i, even as I remember it was complicated when I was there. I miss the sun and the sea probably most of all. But I think, too, I miss something that I put there, that isn't really there. A daydream of belonging in my own skin, of finding a cultural home, of being at peace, of not having to work so hard every day to just be, of being young and beautiful and relaxed and beach-happy forever.

That is a fabrication and it's dangerous. No place can bring me that. Only I can bring me that. And I try to appraise, weakened by the uncertainty of being Multiracial, how much of the tourist fable of the islands or "local" post-racial avoidance I've bought into myself.

It occurs to me you could be a visitor in your own life, your whole life, the place where you live, that you call home. A visitor in your own body, your own mind.

I feel a deep pain acknowledging my privilege within this truth. There's so much I didn't get about being a Mixed Race person when I started this work. I assume there's so much I still don't get. I'm glad to be on this journey. But it's not easy, and there are many days, moments, when I debate what it would be like to retreat into my privilege, to be ignorant and complacent again. I snap at myself that this could never happen. *You can't put yourself back to sleep once you've been woke.* Nor should you try, I reprimand disapprovingly.

I feel rooted in the faraway places of my memory, my childhood, and my fantasies. But I search this moment, my passions, my beliefs, my heart, for where I belong. I'm still searching.

There's a Mixed island fairytale about Hawai'i that "mainlanders," including me, have been told and continue to tell ourselves. It's a white dream painted with surfboards, palm trees, bright hibiscus, and light-skinned "hapa" women in bikinis or coconut bras who beckon you to your next relaxing vacation. Where you learn to undo your racism, or pretend it never existed in the first place, cradled in the arms of bewitching Multiracial girls and charming Multiracial children. A dream where the islands never belonged anywhere, or to anyone, other than the "mainland"; where Indigenous struggles are imperceptible, invisible, obliterated.

But it seems to me there's a Mixed island fairytale that's real in Hawai'i too—a utopic Mixed-Race chimera written by haoles, kept in place by the avoidance and complacency of Asian and haole settlers and even Mixed Race people themselves. Where "everyone's mixed," and "hapa" belongs to anyone, Indigenous struggles be damned; where whites are a minority so white supremacy must not be a thing; where a "mainland" analysis about anti-Black/Brown systemic racism doesn't work for a myriad of maybe good reasons but mostly because it's "mainland," which is the worst reason of all.

In my life and work so far I've run across many incubators for a post-racial fiction I despise. A fiction that tries to convince us if we could all just have Mixed Race babies, if we could all just be Mixed, our racial problems would miraculously vaporize. Fiction that uses Mixed bodies for its own manifest purpose while ignoring or even discarding the people who live in those bodies; that, meanwhile, cloaked under a shroud of multiracial mythology, continues to aggrieve everyone else. It's the same fiction that, at the end of the day, delivers white supremacy to our door lightning fast, free of charge, so we'll gorge on what's inside and recycle the soiled, smelly box it came in.

Washington and California, with some of the nation's largest Mixed Race populations, are two of those incubators. But Hawai'i seems to me one of the incubators too. Especially for a Biracial Asian white woman like me. There are geographical nuances it would be hard, or impossible, for me to ever understand, not being from the land. But the story is too familiar to pretend it isn't. And the so-called improbability, I'm told, of the continent and islands ever entering into exchange about this thing called Mixed Race because we're so different or so incompatible—it makes me very sad.

"Colonization is everywhere," points out my Black Filipinx friend in Seattle, "and there will always be struggles for liberation."

This is not a happy book about Hawai'i, but it's not a hopeless one either. It's a conversation I needed to start having about what multiraciality looks like in relationship to gender, geography, land, and colonization. It's a call to recognize the Sovereignty Movement of Native Hawaiians in Hawai'i, the struggles of Native peoples all across the continent, and how Multiracial model-minority myths often drown out those efforts. It's also a call-in for non-Indigenous Asian Mixed people to continue holding our identities in tension, recognizing that we can be marginalized at the same time we can be privileged, so that we must always ask critical questions about the world around us. Because we have a responsibility to keep showing up not only for ourselves, but for others too.

As an Asian Mixed Woman, I don't think I'll ever fully leave Hawai'i, even as I never belonged there in the first place. If I never go again, it will always resurface as others repeatedly assume my body belongs there, or as I remember fantasizing about belonging there. But I can live with that pull at my heart. I can live with the questions, the thinking, the wondering. And at the end of the day, even though the songs are no longer syrupy sweet, their music loud and driving instead, I appreciate much more being disquieted and challenged than being cajoled and placated.

I'm trying to shake off heavy sleep and step forward into this sunny Seattle summer morning, into dishes, dinner, walking the dogs, bills, errands, laundry. Into being a writer, activist, mother, partner. Into living this life, in this moment, in this place where I really live. It's time to start this day.

Goodbye, Hawai'i.

For now.

EPILOGUE

I am not Kānaka Maoli, and it is a fragile, delicate thing to write about a group you are not part of, particularly when you have participated in the oppression of that group. As a Woman of Color living under white supremacy on the continent, I understand only too well what such power imbalance can look and feel like. In this memoir, I necessarily explored many isms—racism, sexism, colonialism, militarism, imperialism, and more, and it is important to call out these oppressive systems.

But in writing about Hawai'i as a non-Hawaiian writer, there is always risk of portraying Native Hawaiians as victims or passive recipients of those systems rather than as active participants and agents of social change negotiating shifting matrices of power. As a friend and brilliant scholar kindly reminded me upon reading this manuscript: it is true that Native Hawaiians have been colonized, that Hawai'i is a settler colony, and that Hawaiians are dispossessed. It is also true that there is much vitality and resistance happening within Kānaka Maoli communities, and that today there is a full, vibrant Hawaiian cultural and political renaissance taking place.

As this book comes to its conclusion, then, and you are about to close the cover on its final pages, I feel it is critical to reiterate my message from its opening. Please do not *let* this be the end; know that it is not right for my words to be the last. You, the reader, now have a responsibility—to go seek out the excellence of Kānaka Maoli (if you have not done so already) and to ever remember the resilience and brilliance of Indigenous people thriving all over the world.

SELECTED BIBLIOGRAPHY

Camper, Carol, ed. *Miscegenation Blues: Voices of Mixed Race Women*. Toronto: Sister Vision, 1994.

Enomoto, Joy. "Why Black Lives Matter In the Hawaiian Kingdom" (blog post). *Ke Kaʻupu Hehi ʻAle*, February 1, 2017. https://hehiale.wordpress.com/2017/02/01/where-will-you-be-why-black-lives-matter-in-the-hawaiian-kingdom (retrieved May 3, 2018).

Fujikane, Candace, and Jonathan Y. Okamura, eds. *Asian Settler Colonialism: From Local Governance To the Habits of Everyday Life In Hawaiʻi*. Honolulu: University of Hawaiʻi Press, 2008.

Gonzalez, Vernadette Vicuña, *Securing Paradise: Tourism and Militarism in Hawaiʻi and the Philippines*. Durham and London: Duke University Press, 2013.

Goodyear-Kaʻōpua, Noelani, Ikaika Hussey, and Erin Kahunawaikaʻala Wright, eds., *A Nation Rising: Hawaiian Movements for Life, Land, and Sovereignty*. Durham and London: Duke University Press, 2014.

Hall, Dana Naone. *Life of the Land: Articulations of a Native Writer*. Honolulu: ʻAi Pōhaku Press, 2017.

Hara, Marie, and Nora Okja Keller, eds. *Intersecting Circles: The Voices of Hapa Women in Poetry and Prose*. Honolulu: Bamboo Ridge Press, 1999.

Hune, Shirley, and Gail M. Nomura, eds. *Asian/Pacific Islander American Women: A Historical Anthology*. New York: New York University Press, 2003.

Kina, Laura, and Wei Ming Dariotis, eds. *War Baby / Love Child: Mixed Race Asian American Art*. Seattle: University of Washington Press, 2013.

Kuwada, Bryan Kamaoli. "We Are Not Warriors. We Are a Grove of Trees" (blog post). *Ke Ka'upu Hehi 'Ale*, July 6, 2015. https://hehiale.wordpress.com/2015/07/06/we-are-not-warriors-we-are-a-grove-of-trees (retrieved April 19, 2018).

Matsuda, Mari J., ed. *Where Is Your Body? And Other Essays on Race, Gender and the Law*. Massachusetts: Beacon Press, 1996.

Queen Lili'Uokalani. *Hawaii's Story by Hawaii's Queen*. Honolulu: Mutual Publishing, 1991.

Silva, Noenoe K. *Aloha Betrayed: Native Hawaiian Resistance to American Colonialism*. Durham: Duke University Press, 2004.

Trask, Haunani-Kay. *From a Native Daughter: Colonialism and Sovereignty in Hawai'i*, rev. ed. Honolulu: University of Hawai'i Press, 1999.

Trask, Haunani-Kay. "Settlers of Color and 'Immigrant' Hegemony: 'Locals' in Hawai'i." *Amerasia Journal* 26, no. 2 (2000): 1–24.

ABOUT THE AUTHOR

SHARON H. CHANG is an award-winning author, photographer, and activist with a lens on racism, social justice, and the Asian American diaspora. Her writing has appeared in BuzzFeed, ThinkProgress, Racism Review, *Hyphen* magazine, *ParentMap* magazine, South Seattle Emerald, Seattle Globalist, and International Examiner. She was named 2015 Social Justice Commentator of the Year by the Seattle Globalist and selected 2016 Favorite Local API Author/Writer by International Examiner readers. In 2016, she was also awarded First Place, Small Print: Editorial & Commentary by the Society of Professional Journalists Western Washington. *Hapa Tales* is Sharon's second book. She is currently working on a third book looking at Asian American women, gender, and race to be coauthored with preeminent sociologist Joe R. Feagin.

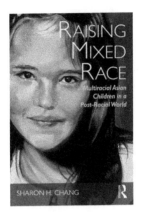

Raising Mixed Race: Multiracial Asian Children in a Post-Racial World

Drawn from extensive research and interviews with sixty-eight parents of multiracial children, *Raising Mixed Race* is the first book to examine the complex task of supporting young children who are "two or more races" and Asian while living among today's deceptive post-racial ideologies.

Routledge / ISBN: 978-1138999466

"This book is groundbreaking. I can't say enough good things about it."

— MINELLE MAHTANI
Author of *Mixed Race Amnesia: Resisting the Romanticization of Multraciality*